SWARTHMORE LECTURE 1960

THE SWARTHMORE LECTURES

VC gift

SWARTHMORE LECTURE 1960

THE CREATIVE
IMAGINATION

BY

KENNETH C. BARNES

LONDON
GEORGE ALLEN & UNWIN LTD
MUSEUM STREET

FIRST PUBLISHED IN 1960
SECOND IMPRESSION 1960
THIRD IMPRESSION 1961

© *George Allen & Unwin Ltd. 1960*

PRINTED IN GREAT BRITAIN
in 11 point Baskerville type
BY HEADLEY BROTHERS LTD
109 KINGSWAY LONDON WC2
AND ASHFORD KENT

PREFACE

The Swarthmore Lectureship was established by the Woodbrooke Extension Committee at a meeting held December 7th, 1907; the minute of the Committee providing for "an annual lecture on some subject relating to the message and work of the Society of Friends". The name "Swarthmore" was chosen in memory of the home of Margaret Fox, which was always open to the earnest seeker after Truth, and from which loving words of sympathy and substantial material help were sent to fellow-workers.

The Lectureship has a twofold purpose; first, to interpret further to the members of the Society of Friends their Message and Mission; and, secondly, to bring before the public the spirit, the aims and the fundamental principles of the Friends. The Lecturer alone is responsible for any opinions expressed.

The Lectures have usually been delivered at the time of the assembly of London Yearly Meeting of the Society of Friends. The present Lecture, in abridged form, was delivered at Friends House, Euston Road, on the evening of May 27th, 1960.

A list of previous Lectures, as published in book form since 1940, will be found at the beginning of this volume, and those prior to 1940 at the end.

BIOGRAPHICAL NOTE

KENNETH BARNES (who became a member of the Society of Friends by convincement in 1920) was born in Battersea in 1903 and educated at elementary schools, Emanuel School, King's College (London) and Woodbrooke. He subsequently taught science at Sheffield Central Secondary School before becoming Senior Science Master at Bedales in 1930. With Frances Barnes he founded Wennington School, of which he is headmaster, in 1940. He was President of the Friends' Guild of Teachers in 1952 and, apart from contributions to Educational and Quaker periodicals, has published *Sex, Friendship and Marriage* (with Frances Barnes), 1938 and *He and She*, 1958.

FOREWORD

One whose job it is to educate has more need than most others to frame a philosophy that will hold his work together. But a boarding school headmaster who is also a teacher of science has his time torn into fragments; he can reflect and write only in odd moments. In these circumstances, to tackle so ambitious a topic as the subject of this essay must inevitably result in many loose ends, and I became specially conscious of the effrontery of my effort when, towards the end of the work, I began to look at Michael Polanyi's book on a related topic—*Personal Knowledge*—the result of nine years' single-minded attention.

What understanding of philosophy I have I owe almost entirely to a long friendship with John Macmurray, in which, however, I have played no more than a humble *Meno* to his *Socrates*. When so many other eminent philosophers have ceased to "battle with dragons" and have become preoccupied with dictionaries, it has been good to have the constant stimulus of one whose thoughts have a positive and immediate relevance to one's daily life and work. The philosophic thread that runs through my essay is to be found fully described in his *The Self as Agent*, in which the "*Cogito ergo sum*" of Descartes, the assumption underlying so much of Western culture, is dismissed and the centre of gravity in philosophy shifted from thought to action. We are primarily doers who "stop to think"; we are not primarily thinkers who act our thoughts. Chapters

II and III of Macmurray's book are specially relevant to the discussion of imagination and dualism, but I have refrained from quoting because every passage contains and implies so much more than I have attempted to deal with.

I have found occasion to criticize orthodox religion, sometimes vigorously, so let me hasten to acknowledge what I owe in Christian encouragement to such men as William Temple and Charles Raven, and F. A. Cockin, until recently Bishop of Bristol, whose broadcasts to Sixth Forms have been a delight. Their work leaves me with a great respect for the freedom and fertility of the Anglican Compromise. A grateful acknowledgement is due also to J. B. Phillips and E. V. Rieu, whose new translations have done so much to reveal meanings and to liberate religious thought from the limitations of traditional phraseology. This has special relevance to the content of Chapter VI.

But none of those whose names I mention, nor of those whom I quote in the essay, should be held responsible for my errors or my possible misuse of their words.

To my wife I owe the opportunity to discuss every idea that comes into my head, with the certainty that it will emerge much less crude as a result of her frank and informed criticism. She has been my Concordance and my Commentary.

K.C.B.

CONTENTS

WHAT IS IMAGINATION?

THOSE who have followed with interest the developments in science of the last twenty years cannot fail to have been impressed by the great surge forward, not only in material achievements but also in theoretical understanding and fertility of ideas. To the scientist this is an immensely exciting time in which to be alive, and to young men and women science offers not only opportunities for solid achievement in a world that now respects science, but also an encouragement to a great expansion of thought. There never was a more fascinating period, especially to those concerned with astrophysics and cosmology, or the chemistry of the living cell explored by the electron microscope. A good teacher of science, aware of what is happening in these fields, can be sure of the rapt attention of his classes. An outstanding feature of the present situation is the evidence of great imaginative activity in the scientist and the stimulus to the imagination in those who are learning about what is happening. In this essay I shall try to discover something of what has made possible this great success of scientific activity and to consider whether in our religious thought and activity we can learn something from it. I believe that we need in religion a new release of imagination comparable to what we are seeing in science, and I want to ask how that could be made possible.

There is evidence, for instance, in the reactions of

various people to Sir Charles Snow's Rede Lecture on *The Two Cultures*, that there are fairly large groups of people who have failed to come to terms with science, who are afraid of it, who see in it a menace—a dark cloud spreading over culture—and who, by reason of their state of mind, cannot see anything of the wholesome fascination and delight so widely experienced by research workers.

There are some among such people whose interest is mainly in religion, but there are also some concerned with the arts and with literature who see in science a threat to their way of life and sensibility. These tend to create the division of culture that they deplore. I believe that this hostility or revulsion is unjustified and I want at the outset to beg for an attitude that fully accepts science and is prepared to learn from it.

I cannot claim to speak at first hand for the research worker; for thirty-five years I have been teaching what other people have discovered. My intellectual training was that of a scientist and the scientific approach asks for a place in all my thinking. More of my time, however, is concerned with education in general than with science teaching, and the problems that I meet from day to day are very different from those in the laboratory. I do not expect to make every decision or judgment on a scientific basis, but I am unready to admit that there is any activity of mankind from which scientific thinking should be wholly shut out. All my interests—and these include the arts—find a place in the life of a school, but they all have to give place to and serve the main interest in the individual boy or girl. If a teacher is really concerned with education his whole self is involved and with it every item of knowledge and skill, every aspect of understanding. To meet human need he must reach down to the limit of his inner resources. Because the educator is concerned as a whole person with the whole child and the whole of man's heritage, he cannot be content with a dichotomy of culture. One subject or one approach may challenge another, but any kind of hostility or repudiation between activities is intolerable.

Perhaps I should begin by considering the kind of situation that an educator has to meet every day. I think this will lead straight to the central thought of this essay—the significance of imagination. Further, because it is a human situation it should be within everyone's experience. A pupil stands before me: it may be a sixteen-year-old boy tied up in an adolescent tangle or a nine-year-old fatherless girl who delights to be picked up, whirled around and hugged. Primarily each is an individual human being, to be accepted and enjoyed even while presenting a problem or manifesting a need. It is almost true to say that I can do nothing for my pupils unless I enjoy them, enjoy them not in any idealistic or mystical sense or for what they might become, but simply as fellow human beings significant in themselves. That is one kind of relationship.

But then I stand back as a spectator of the school and see the surging energy of youth, its ecstasy and its blundering, its sometimes painful struggle towards maturity, and its obvious need of help. I try to assess my own values as an educator and try to discover how I play my part. I think of myself faced with a human situation—a child in difficulty or trouble—and I can descry two processes going on in me. One is intense

3

thought—a searching round for a category in which to put the problem, so that I can do what I have done in similar instances. This involves a strenuous effort to analyse the components, discriminate all the details. General theories of psychology and human motivation may set me searching for items in the child's experience that will explain his present condition.

But at the same time, or alternating with the process I have described, I feel compassion—a compassion that so to speak loosens up my thought into something more imaginative, prompts me to speak to the child as a fellow human being, not the subject of an investigation. This may act in a direct positive way on the relationship and it may bring to light facts that would otherwise be inaccessible.

This is for me an exceedingly important point. The facts about human beings as *human* beings, can only be known in human relationship. To attempt to be completely detached is to make oneself useless and the teacher or psychiatrist who claims such a state is suffering from illusions about himself. What we *can* do is to control the nature of our involvement, so that it really does lead us to knowledge.

A characteristic of human problems is that they are always new; no intimate human situation is quite like its predecessor. Every human situation requires some degree of readjustment from those who try to direct it. We have to *give* something to it before we can do anything effective about it. Scientific or rational principles insensitively applied are never enough—nor even are religious principles or concepts. There is only one word which seems to cover what we have to give in order to understand and act effectively, and that is

4

imagination. If I think of the occasions when I have acted effectively they are occasions when I have acted not only with intelligence and experience, but also imaginatively. If I think of my failures, they are often instances of a failure of imagination. If we put aside the concept of intelligence implied by intelligence tests and think of intelligence in a complete context of thought and action, it is inseparable from imagination.

Think again of the kind of situation in which a schoolteacher often finds himself. He is confronted with a difficult child—obtuse, rebellious, insolent or cynical—and he fails, not necessarily because he is without patience or love, but because his imaginative perception of what lies behind the child's condition and of what is possible in the relationship is not adequate. He cannot reach the child and so he gets no response. He has to dismiss him with judgment or advice couched in conventional phrases, knowing that it is useless.

What I am going to say in this lecture will be mainly about creative imagination and the part it should play in religious experience and expression. It is a distinguishing characteristic of human beings that they can think what has never been thought before and create what has never been made before, so that their experience is ever-expanding.

It seems that little attempt has been made in philosophy or psychology to define imagination. But some of the uses of the word can be discriminated. There is a very restricted use, implying little more than the "having" of an image, which can be the visual image or auditory image produced by something we experience, or an image made up in some way by the mind,

5

a memory image or an hallucination, but nevertheless corresponding to something real or perceivable. Further there is the activity of image-forming in which the images are not of perceivable objects, for instance Pan, with a man's body on the legs of a goat. There is the image-forming tendency emphasized in Gestalt Psychology, in which the mind is put into a state of tension by an uncompleted pattern, for instance a circle with a small portion missing, and tends to bridge the gap and see the complete pattern. This has a wide application, far beyond graphic pattern-forming.

Further, there is an activity of imagination in which "image" is partly or wholly metaphorical, covering any kind of constructive mental activity or any *supposal* from the propositions of algebra to the archetypes of the Jungian unconscious. In this there seems no limit to what the mind can suppose. There is nothing to prevent us supposing that the moon were made of green cheese or that donkeys could speak English.

There is, however, far more mystery than we usually assume in even the simple having of an image. Looking at a rose, having an image of it on the retina and saying "That is a rose" is far more complicated than a comparison with a camera would suggest. Imagination in a wider and more mysterious sense may be involved. The physiologist or psychologist will refer to "sense-data"—the messages that come from the retinal receptors and arrive at their end-points in the brain. But is he referring to anything more than a chemical or electronic disturbance? Can it mean anything in terms of human experience until the mind (whatever that may be!) has provided a sort of framework of significance built up by imagination so that, for

6

instance, if we have a rose in our hands, redness or smell *mean* something?

A. N. Whitehead, writing of Locke and the scientific philosophy that grew out of the 17th century, shows how Locke gave an objective reality to the mass and magnitude—extension in Newtonian space—of bodies, but found other qualities to be subjective. Whitehead, paraphrasing Locke, writes, in *Science and The Modern World*.

> But the mind, in apprehending, also experiences sensations which, properly speaking, are qualities of the mind alone. These sensations are projected by the mind so as to clothe appropriate bodies in external nature. Thus bodies are perceived as with qualities which in reality do not belong to them, qualities which in fact are purely the offspring of the mind. Thus nature gets credit which should in truth be reserved for ourselves: the rose for its scent: the nightingale for its song: and the sun for his radiance. The poets are entirely mistaken. They should address their lyrics to themselves, and should turn them into odes of self-congratulation on the excellency of the human mind. Nature is a dull affair, soundless, scentless, colourless; merely the hurrying of material, endlessly, meaninglessly.

Today we are less certain of the objective nature of mass and extension in space; philosophers write of "conceptual" or "perceptual" space, a frame of reference which the mind supplies but which cannot be guaranteed to be a description of objective reality. If perceptual space, and perhaps time also, are frames of reference provided by the mind, they are a product of imagination.

7

Let us consider a simple example—our awareness of a matchbox. Most of us are aware of its dimensions, its "squareness", the red-and-green perhaps of its label, the peculiar smell of the red-phosphorus composition on its side. All of us habitually accept that these characteristics are *there*, in or on the match box. But a few in every hundred of boys and men, like John Dalton,* do not see a red-and-green label; we call these people colour blind, but is there any justification for saying that they are wrong about it and we are right? Even among normally colour-sensitive people there are variations in the relative intensity of colours.

Think of a blind man experiencing the matchbox— and imagine too that he is without a sense of smell; what would he make of it? You might perhaps say, with Locke, that he was experiencing its irreducible primary inherent qualities—mass, measured by its weight, and its extension in space. I am not at all sure, however, that if our blind man had been brought up in Wells's "Country of the Blind" that "extension in space" would mean to him what it means to a blind man brought up, as all blind men in fact are, by people who have sight and whose imagination is altered by that fact. What kind of mathematics—especially geometry—would an all-blind community produce? Would a member of such an all-blind community have a concept of the beginning and end of a road, or geometrical line, as simultaneously existing, when his only experience of it would be to *move along it in time?*

* John Dalton, Quaker pioneer of the Atomic Theory, was colour blind. This condition was investigated and explained by his contemporary, Thomas Young, founder of the Wave theory of Light and also a product, though not a continuing member, of the Society of Friends.

8

Think too of the blind man turning away from the matchbox and then back to it again. Or think of our sighted selves doing this. What is there in this experience to guarantee that it is the same matchbox that we are looking at and that it continued to exist while our eyes or hands were turned away? It seems to me that we fill in the interval with *imagined* or assumed continuity in time, and that is true however much we reduce the interval to see whether a mysterious agency has in the meantime removed the matchbox.

It might be objected that this is absurd, you simply cannot live—act—without the assumption of continuity. It is plain common sense. To which I answer: of course! I would argue that, contrary to the general tendency of intellectual assumption since Plato, *action* is our primary experience. Thought is secondary; it is the negative or reflective aspect of action; it is the result of the difficulty or frustration of action. This philosophical dictum is implied in the common statement "I *stop* to think".

It is when we think, or describe an event, that we fill in the gaps between a series of otherwise disconnected sense-impressions with an imagined continuity. The very simplest experiences, when they are brought into consciousness and subject to reflection, become meaningful only as a result of the imaginative activity of the mind. To observe—to take notice of—is in some measure to experience, and observation therefore implies imagination. No knowledge is possible without an act of synthesis on the part of the knower, some kind of putting together, the imagining of a relationship. There can be no such thing as a "mere" observation, a passive mind receiving an imprint. We bring some-

9

2B

thing of ourselves to the discrimination of the most trivial object in the outside world.

Although I shall deal later with imagination in science, I think I should include here an example suggested to me as illustrating different levels of imaginative activity—the discovery of penicillin. During a holiday, Fleming left in his laboratory at St. Mary's Hospital some dishes of nutrient jelly on which he had been cultivating colonies of staphylococci which appeared as opaque discs on the otherwise clear jelly. Several of these were spoilt during the holiday by the incursion of other germs and by moulds. On his return, instead of at once throwing away the jelly with the greenish mould on it, Fleming noticed that where the mould was in contact with a bacterial colony the opacity of the colony was being *cleared*. The ultimate result was the discovery of a chemical in the mould that cured diseases caused by staphylococci and several other germs.*

It was not, however, an unprepared imagination that led him to this discovery. Fleming observed what others would not have observed because the clearing of an opacity *meant* something at once. He had often cleared the opacity caused by germs in a liquid, by adding a bacterial solvent, for instance tear-drops which contain the agent lysozyme. This experience and many subsequent efforts to discover bactericides prepared him for the series of imaginative leaps leading to the ultimate discovery. The subsequent search by many other chemists through a whole series of different moulds for other therapeutic substances was not an unimaginative activity, for it still contained the im-

* See the full story in André Maurois' *Life of Sir Alexander Fleming*.

plicit *supposal*; "Suppose we try so-and-so. Perhaps it. . ." But because this is of almost routine quality among research workers it cannot be put in the same class as Fleming's discovery.

I have made what must seem a discursion in order to make it clear that imagination is not an irrational intruder into what would otherwise be "factual" thinking. Some measure of it is there always and inevitably, and at the start. Imagination is not necessarily going beyond the facts into a world of suspect mental processes; without imagination no facts are even presented to the mind. This can be further realized when we consider how, in order to understand a new experience, we deliberately remember past experiences, call them up in verbal or visual images to see how the new experience can be related to them; and how we select past experiences in an imagined pattern in order to predict what will be the result of an action in the future.

Now let me return to the wider concept of imagination necessary in education, either where it concerns intellectual activity or more "whole" experience, reminding the reader that this is a necessary preliminary to what I want to say about the work of Jesus and our understanding of him.

The most recent discussion of imagination in relation to education is to be found in Professor Walsh's essay on "Coleridge and the Age of Childhood",* in which he brings together Coleridge's extraordinarily perceptive statements about imagination from his various writings. Those who wish to understand the educational implications should not fail to read this essay. For

* William Walsh: *The Use of Imagination*. Chatto and Windus 1959.

present purposes I can pick out only a few outstanding remarks.

> .... imagination, the power by which the child prises himself free from the present and loosens the clutch of the immediate. In the imaginative act the child disengages himself from the partial and the broken, "from the universe as a mass of little parts", and comes to conceive of a larger unity and the more inclusive whole. The now is extended, the here complicated. The pressure of the momentary is relaxed and the actual charged with the possible.

Referring to the inadequate idea of imagination as being only concerned with the sense of the aesthetic, he goes on:

> But imagination is not a garnish of the soul, a mere finish according to a fashionable specific. "The rules of the imagination are themselves the very powers of growth and production" . . . imagination is the air in which new knowledge breathes, as it is the salt preserving the savour of the old. "Knowledge", it has been said, "does not keep any better than fish."*

Later in the essay an important and interesting point emerges which has direct relevance to the problem of religious expression which I shall deal with in this lecture. It is also a reminder of what I have said about a blind man's imagery.

In Coleridge's view a main end of education is to rescue the child from the "despotism of the eye", a result to be achieved by cultivating in the child a greater consciousness in the *use of words*† (my italics).

---

* William Walsh, op. cit., pp. 22 and 23.
† In connection with this William Walsh points out how Coleridge anticipated the modern psychologists in noting the primacy of the

These quotations imply that the significance of imagination is universal in human activity. It is often thought that certain activities are imaginative and others are not, that art, poetry, music and novel writing are imaginative but that science and mathematics are purely logical. It has been only in the last decade or so that the importance of imagination in scientific thinking has been definitely recognized, in the sense that writers have given it official recognition in the methodology of science; though of course it has been casually observed or taken for granted often enough. It is interesting that Coleridge made it explicit.

> In the imagination of man exist the seeds of all moral and scientific improvement; chemistry was first alchemy, and out of astrology sprang astronomy. In the childhood of those sciences the imagination opened a way, and furnished materials, on which the ratiocinative powers in a maturer age operated with success.

---

sense of touch, the sense of vision acquiring meaning only by the recollection of touch.

The philosophical implication of this, and the falsification of many treatments of sense perception through a failure to recognize it, are dealt with in John Macmurray's *The Self as Agent* (Faber 1957). Getting to know the environment by touch is obviously active. We *do* something in order to know. It is because with increasing experience we tend to substitute vision—sense awareness at a distance—that we begin to assume that observations can be passive. There is an interesting detailed discussion of the problem in the appendix to *Studies in the History and Methods of the Sciences* by A. D. Ritchie.

13

II

FREEDOM AND IMAGINATION
IN SCIENCE

Now what is science? Often it has been said that
science is a body of established truth. This means a
mass of information that has been confirmed by a
multitude of workers and written down in books. This
might be called the text-book approach to science, and
it is responsible for the too great reverence that many
science students have for text-books. It is a false view of
science, or at the best a most inadequate one. Science
does not rest in text-books. No—it does *rest* in text-
books! It comes to a standstill therein; it dies in the
text-books and it does not come to life again until it
gets out of the text-books and into action. Words in text-
books are meaningless jumbles of black marks until they
re-enter an active mind. Then they begin to mean
something in terms of an activity. I would say that
science is primarily a kind of *activity*. Essentially it is
something that goes on in laboratories, and by that
word I mean not only laboratories as we know them,
but any place inside or outside four walls, including the
Jodrell Bank radio-telescope receiving high frequency
waves from a distant star, a bathysphere deep in the
ocean, an artificial satellite hurled into space and the
great areas of East Africa surveyed by locust-control
investigators. Text-books are merely a means of communication between people interested in a common
activity. Where there are no people there is no science,

no matter how many text-books there are on the shelves.

What are people doing when they are being scientists? They are trying to be objective, to control the environment and make matter do what they will. They are trying to find out what happens to things and living creatures independently of any feelings they, the scientists, may have about what they would *like* to be true. Human beings are capable of great self-deception. The wish can not only be father to the thought, but even responsible for false observations. The boy who is obsessed with ghosts will see a face and a belt and a dagger in a mere wavering shadow, and even a careful scientist can mistake the reading of a voltmeter if he has some idea what value would support the conclusion he is inclined to make. Only when the scientist has achieved a large measure of objectivity can he begin to control matter; indeed he uses this control as a test of how far he has been objective.

There is a further point to be made about science; we must avoid being superstitious about it. There is a prevalent form of superstition of which both the scientist and the layman are often guilty and which is related to reverence for the text-book. It is manifest in such statements as: "Science says that . . ." This superstition consists in believing that there exists some force or authority called "science" that is detached from human beings and that makes pronouncements or threatens our existence. Surely the fact is that all statements are made by scientists, by men, and that what are called authoritative pronouncements are simply statements to which all scientists, or the majority of them, agree.

But science is not just a matter of ascertaining facts; it involves also an activity of the mind in which facts are linked together in an imaginative pattern. Science is highly imaginative and therefore never wholly objective.* Electrons, neutrons, protons, mesons, positrons—these are all creatures of the human imagination, invented to explain how atoms behave, and enabling us to predict how matter *will* behave in any new conditions that we establish. An original creative scientist must be a man who can dream dreams, see patterns forming in his imagination, think and imagine ideas and patterns that no one has ever thought of before and that are *not* given in the facts that he observes.

A recent work devoted to an examination of scientific thinking and giving full place to the contributions to it other than the formal and logical is Beveridge's *The Art of Scientific Investigation.*† He gives instances from the history of the various sciences in which explanations were reached, or important steps forward made, by

---

* The fact that imagination has a place in the simplest observation shows that subjective-objective is little more than a convenience of thought. For an important treatment of this question see the recent massive volume by Prof. M. Polanyi *Personal Knowledge*. On p. 15, referring to the work of Minkowski and Einstein he writes "we cannot account for our acceptance of such theories without endorsing our acknowledgement of a beauty that exhilarates and a profundity that entrances us. Yet the prevailing conception of science, based on the disjunction of subjectivity and objectivity seeks . . . to eliminate from science such passionate, personal human appraisals of theories, or at least to minimize their function to that of a negligible by-play".

He refers later to "indispensable intellectual powers, and their passionate participation in the act of knowing" and to the *personal* co-efficient "which shapes all factual knowledge (and) bridges in doing so the disjunction of subjectivity and objectivity".

It is interesting that throughout this volume Prof. Polanyi freely uses the word *passion* in relation to scientific and intellectual activity, but hardly ever *imagination*.

† Pub. Heinemann 1950.

16

the sudden appearance of an imaginative idea or picture that could not possibly have been inferred logically from known facts. At least one instance—the famous inspiration of Kekulé's benzene ring—points to the value even of relaxed dreaming; and the problem of the fertility of the imagination is seen to depend at least partially on the feeding of it by experience in subjects and activities far removed from science, perhaps music, art, poetry. I mention these points, not only because they are interesting in themselves and have great relevance to educational method, but because every one of them is relevant to the question of how we are to make progress in our religious understanding.

It must be added, imagination must go hand in hand with discipline. To quote A. D. Ritchie,* "The process of imagining has two aspects, good and bad. It may be mere feigning, the road to fraud or lunacy. If this were all, the old rationalists would be right, and we should have to try to use pure reason without imagination; an impossible task." He goes on to show how we must use reason to discipline imagination, but that without imagination there would be nothing to discipline.

The two aspects can be seen in the scientific activities of the 16th and 17th centuries. The scientific revolution of the 17th century came at the end of an age in which the imagination of many supposed searchers for truth was disciplined—if such a term is truly applicable— only by the form of argument favoured by the scholastic philosophers. This kind of disputation was concerned only with logical relationships between statements.

* *Studies in the History and Methods of the Sciences* by A. D. Ritchie.

The statements could be either significant or of no significance whatever, and this sort of thinking, however rigorous in itself, had no means of discriminating between reality and unreality. Anything could be imagined and seriously argued about. It is not surprising that with no anchor to earth fancy floated free, even in the physical sciences. Robert Boyle, writing in the middle of the 17th century, says of the situation:*

> ... a person anything versed in the writings of chymists cannot but discern by their obscure, ambiguous, and almost aenigmatical ways of expressing what they pretend to teach, that they have no mind to be understood at all ...

Boyle worked mainly in the physical sciences where the discipline of experiment was by then widely possible, but William Harvey, half a century before him, is an example of a genius who, because of his time, necessarily had one foot in the new world of experimental science and the other in the world of astrology and alchemy, where grandiose emotive phrases obscured the road to true knowledge.

Harvey lived in a time—the early 17th century—when anatomy, physiology, medicine, were still largely dominated by Galen, whose voluminous works had been regarded for thirteen hundred years with the same respect as that accorded to sacred writings, and to differ with whom was heresy. The stultifying power of this kind of authority can be judged when it is remembered that owing to the ban on human dissection, much of Galen's anatomy was derived from the pig. When the dissection of human corpses became permissible and discrepancies were found, for instance

* *The Sceptical Chymist.*

18

the fact that the human uterus was not bifurcated, it was the corpse that was wrong, not Galen.* His followers in Harvey's time still believed that there was a permeable septum between the right and left ventricles of the heart and that the blood pulsated to and fro like alternating current. We, to whom the continuous circulation of the blood is so simple and obvious an explanation, cannot easily understand what daring imagination was necessary in Harvey to escape from the errors of Galen, so emotionally charged and deeply entrenched was the latter's authority. Harvey's liberated imagination was stimulated and disciplined by observation and experiment. In all this we have the one aspect.

On the other hand, Harvey could write of the blood:†
"The blood, therefore, by reason of its admirable properties and powers, is 'Spirit'. It is also celestial; for nature, the soul, that which answers to the essence of the stars is the inmate of the spirit, in other words, it is something analogous to heaven, the instrument of heaven, vicarious of heaven . . . contained within the veins, however, inasmuch as it is an integral part of the body, and is animated, regenerative, and the immediate instrument and principal seat of the soul, inasmuch, moreover, as it seems to partake of another more divine body, and is transfused by divine animal heat, it obtains remarkable and most excellent powers, and is analogous to the essence of the stars. In so far

* As late as the reign of Henry VIII Galen was regarded as more infallible in medicine than the Pope in the Catholic Church. One young doctor was forced to recant the heresy of imputing error to Galen under pain of expulsion from the Royal College of Physicians. See Raven, *Science, Medicine and Morals.*

† Quoted by Professor James Young in "William Harvey and the Scholastic Tradition" (*British Medical Journal,* October 6th, 1951).

as it is spirit, it is the hearth, the vesta, the household divinity, the innate heat, the sum of the microcosm, the fire of Plato."

His *De Generatione Animalium* records a great quantity of accurate observations, but he falls back again on the essence of the stars to explain conception. Conception has nothing to do with the seminal fluid, it is due to a spiritual influence, a divine agency operating at the moment of union. The discipline of the microscope, which had yet to be invented by Malpighi, would have guided his imagination in a different direction, for he would have seen the spermatozoa.

The most recent treatment of the part played by temperament and imagination in the progress of science is Arthur Koestler's *The Sleepwalkers*.* Towards the end of this voluminous, richly documented and intensely interesting work on the history of cosmology, the central and major part of which is concerned with the extraordinary perverted character of Kepler, Koestler reflects on the characteristics that are shared by the geniuses responsible for the major mutations in the history of thought. "On the one hand scepticism, often carried to the point of iconoclasm, in their attitude to traditional ideas, axioms and dogmas, towards everything that is taken for granted; on the other hand an open-mindedness that verges on naïve credulity towards new concepts which seem to hold out some promise to their instinctive gropings. Out of this combination results that crucial capacity of perceiving a familar object, situation, problem, or collection of data, in a sudden new light or new context ... The discoverer perceives relational patterns or func-

* Pub. *Hutchinson* 1959.

tional analogies where nobody saw them before, as the poet perceives the image of a camel in a drifting cloud.

"This act of wrenching away an object or concept from the habitual associative context and seeing it in a new context is, as I have tried to show, an essential part of the creative process . . . Every creative act—in science, art or religion—involves a regression to a more primitive level, a new innocence of perception liberated from the cataract of accepted beliefs. It is a process of *reculer pour mieux sauter*, of disintegration preceding a new synthesis, comparable to the dark night of the soul through which the mystic must pass."

In writing thus he is thinking of the great difficulties, not of reason, but of imagination, that had to be overcome before Newton's great synthesis could bring together the known facts about the heavenly bodies into a satisfying inclusive theory. In this, Newton had to accept in imagination what his reason rejected: gravity, a force acting at a distance through empty space. To others this had been an impossibility. His great contemporary, Descartes, had to imagine space filled with eddies and vortices which, in actual contact with the planets, clutched and swirled them along. Kepler filled the distance between sun and planets with ghostly arms, spokes of force, whips or sweeping brooms. What the man-in-the-street accepts today as though no-one could ever have thought otherwise—forces acting at a distance, the moon held in its orbit by gravity, magnetism and static electricity operating across a vacuum—this was unthinkable to the mediaeval mind.

So difficult was it that Newton himself had to say in

3A

his oft-quoted letter to Bentley that it was to him "so great an absurdity that I believe no man who has in philosophical matters a complete faculty of thinking, can ever fall into it". Koestler continues:

> With true sleepwalker's assurance, Newton avoided the booby-traps strewn over the field; magnetism, circular inertia, Galileo's tides, Kepler's sweeping brooms, Descartes' vortices—and at the same time knowingly walked into what looked like the deadliest trap of all: action-at-a-distance, ubiquitous, pervading the entire universe like the presence of the Holy Ghost.

With true sleepwalker's assurance. This is how Koestler sees the operation of genius—the inexplicable leap of the imagination in people who seem hardly to know what they are doing. This is an unfamiliar idea to those who have thought of science as the product of steady upward development. But can there be many people holding such an erroneous idea now—in this present world where a tremendous revolution in scientific imagination has taken place? We have the extraordinary concept of the expanding universe, with ancillary concepts of a pulsating or exploding universe. Our beloved law of the conservation of matter had to go overboard—or become merged into an inclusive law of the conservation of energy. But now, to fill the expanding space of the universe and maintain a steady state we have been asked to imagine the creation of matter and energy out of nothing—the "continuous creation" theory of Bondi, Gold and Hoyle.

As for space and matter, the special and general theories of relativity have left us with what W. B. Bonnor calls "a compromise between the void and the plenum", i.e. between the empty space with action-at-distance of Newton and the filled-in space of Descartes. Modern field-theory sees space filled with the energy of fields of force, and since matter is regarded as a form of energy, this reminds us of the whirls and vortices with which Descartes filled the universe and of his refusal to dissociate space from the extension of matter.

If we substitute "scientist" for poet, we can hardly better Shakespeare's words as a description of the condition of science today.

> And as imagination bodies forth
> The form of things unknown, the poet's pen
> Turns them into shapes, and gives to airy nothing
> A local habitation and a name.

How well this could apply to the physicist's description of fundamental particles! Since I was a student, the beautiful simplicity of proton-and-electron has been displaced by a complex multiplicity: proton, electron, positron, neutron, neutrino, two hyperons and at least seven mesons; and on top of that the concept of anti-matter. Sir James Jeans many years ago thought of God as the Great Mathematician. It has been said more recently and less seriously that God must be the Great Physicist, for as soon as the ordinary human physicist foresees the possibility of a new fundamental particle, God provides one so that he shall not be disappointed.

Much of the foregoing may seem to have been an unnecessary digression into the nature of scientific activity, while the intention of this lecture should be religious understanding and enlightenment. So I must emphasize that I have been examining science precisely because it has proved so successful, because it is so immensely and inevitably significant in our lives. I hope that characteristics will have been revealed that are universal in human thought and action—characteristics which, if we paid more attention to them, might enliven our religious perception and increase our efficiency as religious people.

Let me recall that Koestler, in the passage just quoted, used the phrase: "Every creative act—in science, art *or religion* involves . . . a new innocence of perception liberated from the cataract of accepted beliefs."

III

DISCOVERY IN POETRY AND RELIGION

WHEN we recognize the part played by imagination in science it brings that activity much closer to the other activities of the human mind. Science is then no longer seen as a foreign intruder into our cultural life, using faculties fundamentally different from those used by artists, poets, writers, musicians, historians. It is not surprising that we should discover, in the educational record of some of our greatest scientists evidence that they could have been as great in the arts, had they so chosen.

Lest this should be a very new idea to some of my readers, let me say a word about poetry. The Society of Friends has a remarkable record in the production of scientists; it was estimated from the records that at least up to 1905, a Quaker was 47 times more likely than one of the general public to become a Fellow of the Royal Society. But we have not so good a record in the matter of poetry and the arts. Quaker interest in poetry has been largely pious; for us good poetry has been verse that put into rhymed and metered form religious sentiments that could equally well have been put in prose, but that were more moving when they were versified. This is a very inadequate conception of poetry. Poetry should never be thought of as a versification of prose ideas. Poetry is itself an instrument of discovery, a means of exploration of truth and human experience. It provides a way of penetrating into our own hearts and minds, of discovering in experience depths and subtleties that would never otherwise be apparent to us. It is a way of becoming more observant, more sensitive, more aware of the moving patterns and relationships in and behind experience. It is an activity that has its own intense discipline in which the choice of words leads to a sharpened awareness of the experiences that the words are to express.

Just as in science, so in poetry, there cannot be pattern or relationship without imagination. Here poetry and science meet; both are means to discovery and to both a vivid and daring imagination is a necessity.

This is not to say that science and poetry are one or will converge. Science tends to isolate elements in experience, to detach particular observations from their subjective pattern and make them objectively verifiable. Poetry, like other forms of art, explores the whole subjective pattern, holding it together in its living relationships within the personality. Science strives to be impersonal;* poetry, music and art are deeply personal. But the important point for me at present is what they have in common: imagination and discovery. One important consequence must be observed; in any activity that is in the nature of a discovery we cannot know in advance what the discovery will be, for this would be to make an absurdity of the whole process.

It is not the proper function of poetry, any more than

---

* Note that I have said *strives* to be. There is a sense in which it cannot be impersonal, precisely because of the fact that it is imaginative and a distinctly human activity.

it is the function of science, to confirm our beliefs; if it is true discovery it may compel us to alter them. I have before me a Catholic text-book on education, and in a chapter that seems to fall all too smoothly off the pen of the writer, the teacher is instructed to use literature to support the faith. Reference is made to "correct orientation", to the necessity that what the child reads should harmonize with and supplement what the teacher says, "otherwise truth may come to be regarded as a matter of mere opinion". I would say that it is an abuse of literature to use it in this way, just as it would be of science—indeed it would be the death of science. If we have faith in the unity of God and Truth we should have the courage to follow where truth leads.

It is not a very big step from poetry to religion, for both are concerned with the relation between the subjective and the objective world, what goes on within us and outside us. A great deal of poetry even when it is not overtly religious is in fact religious, and deeply so, because it is concerned with the whole of life and the truth about man in his innermost experiences, and the revelation of the human predicament.

If there is this unity of aim it is to be expected that religious activity will share characteristics with science and poetry. So, I suggest, it does: it depends upon imagination and is directed towards discovery. But when I say discovery I mean real discovery. Most children carrying out chemical experiments in a school laboratory know in advance what the result will be. It is all in the text-book; they are told to notice that chlorine gas is yellowish-green and that it is heavier than air. All too often the adventure of the religious life has been assumed to be like that. If you do not obey the instructions you will not get the right result. You make your mistakes and commit your sins, only to discover that the text-book of virtue was right; you need not have gone astray, for all the characteristics of the good life were known already. This is a poor conception of religion, just as chemistry done in cookery-book fashion conveys a poor conception of science. It is simply not true that all the characteristics of the good life are known already. The deeper the level at which we try to live, the more unexpected and unpredictable our experiences will be. Just as each human being is unique so each truly personal situation is a unique situation; what is right in each situation cannot be known until we are *in* it. Morality even at its best can only be an approximation; beyond that we must seek earnestly and sensitively for the Will of God.

It must be obvious from the Gospels that this was the way Jesus lived. His actual statements about the Law, if they have been correctly reported, are contradictory. At times he seemed to brush the Law aside; at another time he said "one jot or tittle shall in no wise pass from the Law until all be fulfilled".* But it is clear from all the rest of his life and activity that for him fulfilment meant living not by rule but "in the way", with the nearness to God that enabled him to see to the heart of a situation and deal constructively with it, not merely to judge, to appraise, to condemn. It is a tragedy that the Church has attempted so often—in repudiation of the experience of its greatest saints—to standardize religious experience, when in fact Christian experience, precisely because it is per-

* See further reference on page 49.

sonal, must be the very opposite of standardized. There is also the standardization of worship; the Catholic and the Anglican provide a number of stereotyped symbols, the Quakers a collection of overworked phrases. Feeling tends to become attached to these symbols and phrases instead of to people and action. The result is sentiment and sentimentality instead of religion.

This inadequacy has been supported and encouraged by the use of absolute terms in reference to Jesus, describing him as the perfect, complete, final revelation of God, so that he becomes the end of our religious quest instead of the beginning, closing the book and leaving nothing more to be said.

It is always necessary when referring to the perfectionism of Christians to emphasize that to be perfect in the Gospel sense has little in common with perfection in the ordinary sense. In the everyday sense to be perfect is to be faultless, like a carefully drawn circle, to be made exactly to a known pattern, to perform exactly in accordance with demands or rules. In a human being such a condition would be utterly intolerable, in fact inhuman, impossible to live with. Of those who strive towards this, Cecil Day Lewis wrote:*

One wooed perfection; he's bedded deep in the
glacier, perfect
And null, the prince and image of despair.

Yet a great number of Christians unthinkingly accept this conception of perfection and forget that in the time of Jesus those who held it before the public eye were the Pharisees.

* *Overtures to Death* (Cape, 1938).

Perfectionism of the unhelpful sort is seen in the concept of Jesus as the sinless one. To me this is an example of the degradation of personality by the use of categories. It is not a question of whether it is true or untrue to say that Jesus was sinless; in relation to his essential nature it is irrelevant. It adds nothing to our understanding of his significance, but rather introduces an obstacle. Jesus himself gave us a wholly different way of assessing and appreciating personality. I must insist on the continuity of the human and the divine. The significance of our friends to us is not a matter of what virtues they possess and what sins they retain; we do not see their lives as significant in proportion to their virtues and in inverse proportion to their sins. (Nor, it would seem, does God: "He hath not dealt with us after our sins nor rewarded us according to our iniquities.") In the active experience of love we are not concerned with assessment; we are taken far beyond sins and virtues. How can we bring Jesus down to a level of judgment that in human relationship we are taken beyond?

The most helpful suggestion I have heard as to the meaning of the original word translated as perfect is *mature*. What Jesus was saying was "For Heaven's sake grow up! Become mature enough to walk with God." And what more relevant command could we give to the people of the world today than that they should *grow up*?

The false conception of perfection and finality is another example of the way in which men have denied the humanity of Jesus, repudiated the Incarnation and tried to make him fundamentally different from the rest of human beings. If we think of the best of our friends, those whom we respect and love and delight in, with whom we share our intimate thoughts, are those the people who make us feel that we have come to the end of a journey, that there is nothing more to discover or understand? No, they are precisely the people who become our companions rather than objects of adoration, who open up endless possibilities of experience, who help us to be born again into a new world.

IV

APPROACH TO JESUS

I AM convinced that we must, every one of us, subject ourselves now and then to the discipline of bringing ourselves to the story of Jesus as though we had never heard of it before, and putting aside all the authoritative statements that have ever been made about him. We should try to approach the story with the humility of a scientist before his facts, or of a young child looking at life with a fresh uncluttered mind. If we do not do this we shall do as some text-book writers do—copy from each other, encourage second-hand feelings and perpetuate errors.

I am aware that this attempt has its dangers. It could be said that I shall merely select from the Gospels what I want to select to support my own point of view. A Catholic would question my right to set my individual judgment against the tradition and authority of the Church. To this I must answer with the words put into the mouth of Joan of Arc by Bernard Shaw: "What other judgment can I judge by but my own?" Even the decision to submit to the authority of the Church is itself an individual judgment. When the Church, be it Roman or Anglican, insists that the Gospels must be read in the light of Christian doctrine I see an element of fear that sorts ill with Christianity. It is a fear of truth—or rather a fear of what the search for truth will reveal. It is a fear that if—feeble creatures that we are—we pursue the search for truth independently we shall be misled by the Devil. There are explosive elements in the Gospels of which the Church has always been afraid—like radioactive material that has to be shut up in leaden coffins.

It is in ways like this that the Church, in spite of its firm logical repudiation of the heresies, is always tending to tumble backwards into the Manichean heresy. If this is God's world, not a world in which God and Devil are equally matched, then the independent search for truth, carried out with the humility and discipline that science, for instance, brings to its work, cannot but lead us to God.

Beginning thus, I see Jesus as the people of his time must have seen him to begin with, primarily as a man, a fellow human being, but one who produced in his friends and listeners an intense awareness. He was concerned to show people what human life *is* in all its aspects and dimensions, to show them what possibilities there are in human nature when it reaches towards the divine—towards maturity—to show them how they could know their own powers, how they could cease to be the victims of circumstances and their oppressors, how, through understanding, they could direct their lives and control their destiny.

In his feeling I see him supremely as a man of compassion. That is, he entered into every aspect and event of human life, knowing it in its truth and reality, sharing all that human beings experienced, not only perceiving what men and women felt, but feeling with them. With those who needed tenderness he was tender, but his love was not always gentle. He would not spare people the truth, even when it had to hurt. He could love the rich young man and yet say to him that he could not inherit eternal life if he did not give up his riches. He flayed the oppressors of the poor with the most biting invective that has ever been used. His love could be gentle, but it could also be stern and austere, intensely demanding.

I see him deeply involved in the conflict of his time, not standing aside offering advice or principles from on high, but deeply involved, right *in* the conflict, followed round by contentious groups, supported or attacked, applauded or derided, loved or feared. He was a man of passion, not only in his suffering, but throughout his life and ministry. I do not see him as a preordained sacrifice, appointed by the Father to go through these earthly experiences and to die as he did in order to expiate the sins of man, a symbolic gesture, to pay back a debt to a righteous God.

There is no doubt that Jesus came to look upon himself as one whose task it was to fulfil the act of creation which God had begun among the Jewish people. In the Galilean community into which he was born there was an encouragement to accept leadership. But his assumption of a messianic mission was a responsible personal decision, a deliberate act of creation, not an acquiescent fulfilment of a plan. The messianic prophecies in the Old Testament are contradictory, couched in poetic terms; the temptations show how these strains conflicted: the bread provider, the Son of Man of Daniel's vision descending from Heaven, the conquering King. He had to choose.

The later writers, Matthew and John, unlike Mark, make frequent claims such as: "For these things were done that the Scripture should be fulfilled." This was an effort to convince the Jews of a continuity

34

of tradition, but it appears like a statement of causality or intention. The fact is that the fulfilment when it came was totally unexpected. For indeed, what the Jewish people found among them was in no recognizable sense a fulfilment of prophecy. They expected a strong man and a deliverer, a man of distinction and power. What they got was first a baby born in humble circumstances, and later a blasphemer from a district of ill repute: "Can any good thing come out of Nazareth?"

Because he dared to live a life of truth and love in a world riddled with falsehood and evil, he could not help but call upon himself all the hatred and fear of those who could not stand the light, those who could not meet his demands for an utter purging of their personal and social life. His suffering was not arranged in order to demonstrate his love; it was a sheer consequence of it.

For him, love necessarily involved an attack, indeed an unrelenting war, on all that stood in the way of love, that shut off man from man, a war on greed, wealth, privilege, power, cruelty and corruption, and perhaps more than anything else on hypocrisy—the assumption of goodness that covered exploitation and cunning. He could have talked of love, as many mistaken Christians talk of it today, as something to keep everyone happy, a soothing magic to prevent trouble. But love and truth were inseparable to Jesus. Truth broke out fiercely from his lips; and so he had to die.

You will perhaps be thinking that I am making too much of Jesus in his manhood, Jesus as Man. But it is the very depth and completeness of his manhood that speak to me of his divinity. To me the most moving words he ever spoke were not words of confidence; they were not part of his teaching or of his gospel. They were the words he spoke when, in the intensity of his suffering, his faith began to break. "My God, my God; why hast thou forsaken me?" In these words he identified himself with everyone whose faith is tried to the breaking point, with all the mute sufferers throughout history who have been scourged into submission, who have been broken on the wheel, torn on the rack or crowded into gas chambers, also with every one of us when by death or separation we suffer the almost intolerable loss of those we love, making us wonder whether God really cares.

I have said that it is the completeness of his manhood that convinces me of his divinity. Isn't that exactly what one would expect? It sounds paradoxical—but don't we in fact assess our friends in precisely the same way? Those who plumb human life to its depths, who feel *human* experience in its greatest intensity, are precisely those who help us to know God.

The scientific approach involves questioning everything that can be questioned, until we discover that which cannot be doubted. Following this in relation to Christianity brings me to a point where I am sharply aware of the firm point on which I stand. There is a convincing unity between Jesus, in so far as I can know him, and the experience of human life. Even though what is recorded of him is fragmentary, it is an inexhaustible source of stimulation and understanding in relation to our own life. He shows us what God is like and he also shows us what life is like. We have too much thought of him as one who exhorts us, urges us, beckons us, tells us what we ought to think and feel and do. We have too little recognized that he shows us what life *is*, and what we *are*, that he is saying: *this is the truth: you neglect it at your peril.* Jesus was nearer to the scientist than to the moralist.

Not only do I feel that in my perception of Jesus I find the firm basis of my faith, but also I see in what he did, something very akin to what the scientist does. Jesus was a man who expressed love, tenderness, compassion, mercy, but he also asked people to face the truth. He was objective. He demanded that the people of his time should dig themselves out of what H. G. Wells, in a very fine passage about Jesus,* calls the *snug burrows* they had lived in hitherto—burrows built out of prejudice, complacency, superiority, self-righteousness, and all the other forms of subjectivity. He demanded that they should face the truth about life, about the evil in their own hearts and the corruption of their community. He allowed himself no false comforts, no illusions, no baseless optimism; eventually he began to know where his actions would lead and what the end would be. There came a point where he asked that, if it were part of God's way with the world, he might be spared the final suffering, "Father, if it be possible, let this cup pass from me." But he asked for no miraculous rescue, no reprieve that was not of the nature of life as lived by his fellow men. He died rejected and despised, mocked and spat upon.

I spent several days in Jerusalem two years ago. It was an interesting but not always happy experience. A shell-torn no-man's-land a few yards from the Church of the Holy Sepulchre; barbed wire and guard

* *Outline of History* (Cassell).

4A

posts; Jew and Arab looking at each other across that no-man's-land with hostility—over rifles and sten guns. It was a poignant reminder of human failure and perversity on the very spot where Jesus died to give us life. There were, as you can imagine, many churches in Jerusalem, but as I walked through them they could do nothing to make me feel that the message of Jesus had been understood even by his professed followers. In all those churches I saw great oil-paintings, paintings of the Crucifixion, every one of them insipid and sentimental; Jesus the pitiable acquiescent sacrifice. They seemed to me to portray a lie, a lie that has been fostered by churches of almost every denomination, the lie that has taken the fire out of Christianity. I cannot believe that Jesus died as an acquiescent sacrifice; it seems to me a perverted notion. To me, he died as a strong man dies, at war with overwhelming odds and deserted by his own followers, died not in the sure knowledge that he was serving God's purpose, but desperately holding off the fear that God too was deserting him. As I have said, it is in this that he comes nearest to me, for this is the fear of all mankind, the fear in the heart of every one of us.

Within an extraordinarily short time the "good news" was sweeping through the Roman world, bringing faith, joy and a sense of significance to the oppressed, and an intense awareness of the personality of Jesus at work among them, an awareness of triumph over disaster. The extent of this triumph cannot be recognized if we do not admit the reality and depth of the fear.

As I looked from the Mount of Olives over Jerusalem, where almost every section of the Christian Church

THE CREATIVE IMAGINATION

has fanatically grabbed at a few square yards of earth
on which to stake its claim, I felt that I could not bear
what the Western world has done in the name of
Christ. Nowhere, in all these institutions, did Jesus
belong. I doubt if he would have any less reason to
say today, "The foxes have holes, and the birds of
the air have nests; but the Son of Man hath not where
to lay his head." No, I could not believe that Jesus
belonged there, in any kind of institution, he did not
belong anywhere but in the heart of man, in the love
of people for each other, in communities gathered
together in anxiety or danger, in prison cells and
concentration camps and gas chambers.

This may be overdrawn, but I think that it is the
kind of reaction one must have if one tries to put
oneself back into the situation in which Jesus found
himself, and if one faces the fact that we human beings
of the present day, no matter how great our religious
claims, are prone to the same kind of pride, self-
righteousness and insensitiveness, and the same desire
for authority and power as were the Scribes and
Pharisees of his day. Even when Christians have been
free from these sins, they have tried to build up a
Christianity of safety, the safety of the great institution
and the universal faith. Jesus offered us no safety—
except in the love of God.

V

THE INCARNATION WAS COMPLETE

It will be recognized that in the foregoing I have been emphasizing the great significance for me of the Incarnation. That word has been so much used that for the uninitiated, the bored or the rebellious, it has ceased to have any significance. It is relegated to the apparently magical and superstitious in Christianity. But it simply means that in Jesus, God, hitherto a bodiless voice, a mysterious prompting, a stirring in the heart, became known in completely human form, one with whom men and women could walk and converse, whom they could understand through their own nature and experience, whom they could know intimately and love as he knew and loved them.

Christians look to the suffering of Jesus on the Cross as the principal manifestation of the Incarnation. I imagine that most would share to a large degree the feelings I have described as my own response to the Cross. Next they think of the temptations. "In all points tempted as we are." But how many allow their imagination to perceive what is implied by "in all points" and how many get beyond the symbolism of the three temptations to recognize all that was behind and implied by it?

Often the recognition of the Incarnation stops at the Cross and the temptations. The rest of Jesus's life and activity is too often thought of as, so to speak, arranged for him, planned in advance to accomplish a prophecy and a destiny. His words, it would seem, were not thought out as we think out our statements, but were put into his mouth, and his actions were not the actions of a man who makes real decisions from moment to moment as he watches the course of events, but a man who could not help himself—who was directed. At worst we are given a picture of a man who moved about the stage of Palestine like a puppet moved by strings held in the hands of an unseen power above. In all this I see the impulse, never quite absent from human beings, to believe in magic—the magic that is so much easier to accept than the need to reach understanding through thought and imagination; the magic which, precisely because that is what it is, takes away responsibility and discourages maturity.

In fact the Incarnation must have meant a unity of experience with man *at every point*. I want to suggest some of its less dramatic implications. Wisdom did not come miraculously to Jesus, like Athene springing full grown and fully armed from the head of Zeus. I cannot accept with Aquinas that Jesus knew everything from his conception. Not only would this make all his decisions and choices unreal but would take away the reality of his suffering in the last days; it would reduce it to physical pain—the least significant aspect of human suffering. It makes nonsense of his last despairing cry. I believe, with Cadoux,* that Jesus had expected and hoped for a different ending to his messianic mission, and that the intense focus of his suffering was his awareness of the rejection of his love and the apparent destruction of his hopes.

* C. J. Cadoux. *The Life of Jesus* (Penguin, 1948). A beautifully clear and admirably courageous account.

Jesus, I believe, had to acquire knowledge as we have to acquire it. Through disciplined attention he became supremely aware of the world and his place in it. He was soaked in the knowledge of his people, their history, their tradition, their literature. It was ordered knowledge and it must have been acquired at great cost in labour and self-discipline. He could not have found it easy, reading his own Old Testament library full of contradictory material. Think of all the difficult material in the Pentateuch. Consider how painfully and gradually the concept of the Suffering Servant emerges—how God's will for the Jewish people is seen, so to speak, only through peep-holes. Even the book of Hosea, that most gentle of the prophets, is more than half full of vituperation and anger against the wicked; there is little that points to the possibility of redemption. God is a God of the just and the righteous, not of the wicked. One wonders how long and by what severe discipline Jesus worked through it all to discover how he could fulfil God's intentions.

If we reject the idea that statements came magically from the mouth of Jesus, we must recognize what depth of experience they implied. The Sermon on the Mount must have been, in a sense, autobiographical:

> How happy are the humble-minded, for the Kingdom of Heaven is theirs!
>
> How happy are those who know what sorrow means, for they will be given courage and comfort!
>
> Happy are those who claim nothing, for the whole earth will belong to them!
>
> Happy are those who are hungry and thirsty for goodness, for they will be fully satisfied.

42

> Happy are the merciful, for they will have mercy shown them.
>
> Happy are the utterly sincere, for they will see God.
>
> Happy are those who make peace, for they will be known as the sons of God.
>
> Happy are those who have suffered persecution for the sake of goodness, for the Kingdom of Heaven is theirs.
>
> You are the earth's salt. You are the world's light.
>
> Don't criticise people and you will not be criticised.
>
> Take the plank out of your own eye first, and then you can see clearly enough to remove your brother's speck of dust.
>
> Ask and it will be given you. Search and you will find.
>
> Consider how the wild flowers grow . . . even Solomon in all his glory was never arrayed like one of these!*

All these and the many other things he said were surely not magically conceived in the brain of a precocious young man, but were the product of a deep and intense experience. They were the summing up of an approach to life that carried not only the conviction of clear perception but also the authority of a deeply assimilated and extensive experience.

Moreover, what we read in the Gospels does not suggest that Jesus achieved his knowledge and understanding in the first thirty years of his life and then simply set out to put it into practice. On the contrary it seems that, like us, he had to go on learning. Consider the extraordinary story, recorded in both Mark and Matthew, of the Syro-Phoenician woman. It is so surprising a story that it could not have been invented;

* Translation by J. B. Phillips. I have used this because, although less majestic and poetic than the authorized version, its freshness provokes thought.

43

it must have happened. But to the orthodox it is an embarrassing story; that is perhaps why it is not often referred to. Putting together the two versions, we gather that when Jesus went away into what is now Lebanon he tried to get some privacy, some respite from the demand on his healing resources. But this non-Jewish woman, having discovered where he was, begged that he would heal her mentally afflicted daughter. Jesus turned away from her in silence. His disciples asked him to do something if only to prevent the woman from becoming a nuisance to them; but Jesus said that his mission was only to the lost sheep of the House of Israel. When the woman herself besought him to help her, he said "Shall the children's food be thrown to the dogs?"* Then came that humble plea that makes the story so poignant and so real: "But Master, the dogs eat the crumbs that fall from the children's table."

I do not see how that story can in any way be fitted into a pattern of perfection and omniscience.† It does suggest that half-way through the three years of his appointed task Jesus' view of redemption was still primarily a tribal one and his compassion limited to his own people. Jesus turned away from a woman in distress and called her people dogs. If we put the best interpretation we can on it, a preoccupation with a plan or a mission caused him for a few minutes to put

---

* The term used for "dogs" was that signifying domestic dogs or puppies.

† I have since learned that an orthodox view is that Jesus behaved like this to try the woman's faith. Such a view reminds one of the way certain religious people opposed the concept of evolution by saying that God put the fossils in the rocks to try our faith. Arguments of this kind are scarcely honest and they make any kind of objective thought and discussion impossible.

44

policy before the needs of a person. Perhaps that was another of the great turning points of his life, the moment of the revelation of the universal love of God, an amplification of the revelation during the temptations. It is recorded that he went away into the mountains above Galilee. One can imagine him trying to get a little quiet there to assimilate this extraordinary experience, recognizing that henceforth his message was to the whole world and his compassion open to every sufferer of every nation. That Jesus had to learn the will of God from experience in this way takes away nothing from his significance. On the contrary it is an immense encouragement to know that he had to learn as we have to learn, and to recognize that the greatest vision of all came not by magic or supernatural gift but by a humbling experience such as all of us are bound to suffer. It gives a new depth, a new intimacy to the Incarnation, so that the words of Gerard Manley Hopkins come to one with new conviction, his Catholicism notwithstanding:

> In a flash, at a trumpet clash
> I am all at once what Christ is, since he was what I am,
>   and
> This Jack, joke, poor potsherd, patch, matchwood,
>   immortal diamond
> Is immortal diamond.

Does it take away anything from the significance of Jesus to say that he was intelligent? For me that is another element in the Incarnation. A high intelligence is not necessary to an understanding of the truth of personal life and relationship—but intelligence was necessary to the kind of life Jesus lived, in which the cleverest of the Jewish people were often pitted against him and only a brilliant intelligence could have enabled him to be effective. Not only did his attackers realize that he spoke with a spiritual authority that overawed them, but that they dare not become involved in argument with him. Can I say too that he was astute? He was at the focus of a strategy and he knew it—a strategy, to trick him, to trip him up, to discredit him in the light of tradition and law. But he was not going to be tripped up while there was still hope, still work to be done. He turned the questions back on the questioners, not as in a mere debate, to score off them, but in such a way as to make them search their hearts. "Render unto Caesar that which is Caesar's and unto God that which is God's" is not an order but the posing of an eternal question. So perhaps is: "Whom God hath joined let no man put asunder." How much *do* we owe to Caesar—ever? When and where *does* God join man and woman—at the high altar, in Hollywood, at the blacksmith's anvil or the heart of the jungle? Is God always and necessarily present in a Friends' Meeting?

Is there any reason why we should not see Jesus as one of the great persons in history whom we think of as men of genius? For me this is simply another inevitable aspect of the Incarnation. What does it mean to say that he was a genius? It meant a tremendous power of penetration and creativeness, a kind of incandescence in which the whole personality is lit up by the energy passing through it. And it implies an exceptionally fertile, disciplined imagination.

I have tried to explain that there can be no knowledge without imagination, without our putting into our perception of an object something that is not given in the object itself. All knowledge involves a putting together. If this is true Jesus could never have responded to situations in a ready-planned way. The wisdom of God could never have been a response known in advance; it must have come into existence with the situation to which it was a response. The divine wisdom was not, so to speak, implied in the primordial atom but is a matter of continuous creation.

The living, ever-new quality of the gospel, its power to evoke interest and response, can be said to arise from the richness and imagination that Jesus put into his teaching. Tidy logical replies to the many questions put to him would never have survived and they would have given us but a fraction of the truth. Think of the way he made his points by parables. The parable evokes—raises in our own imagination—far more than an authoritative logical statement can do. It does not clinch an argument but causes thought to proliferate. Parables can have several depths of meaning and in this they show the characteristics of poetry at its greatest. Think of the fecundity of imagination shown in such parables as those of the Kingdom and of the depth of meaning in the greatest parable of all—that of the prodigal son—into which it is possible to read the whole predicament of Israel.

In view of the richness of metaphor, poetry and parable throughout the sayings of Jesus it seems absurd that the interpretation of his statements during the Last Supper should ever have been a matter of contention among Christians. In saying "This is my body . . . this is my blood" Jesus was doing what he had been doing all his adult life, using symbol and metaphor in speaking to a people for whom these were the everyday currency of speech.* It should be remarked that Jesus also said, "I am the vine and ye are the branches." Why has not the Church taken *that* literally?

I have already explained how there has to be a close relationship between imagination and discipline. It must be a living and reciprocal relationship—for an ill-used discipline can destroy imagination. Poetry does not merely come into the head of a poet—it is a product of sensitiveness and an intense disciplined struggle. The parables were not merely devices for teaching thought up at the moment, however spontaneously they came to the lips of Jesus; they were made possible by a whole lifetime of prayer and effort to understand.

The imaginative person perceives a uniting pattern where the unimaginative perceives only disconnected scraps, and he often discovers below appearances a significance that would otherwise pass unnoticed. We can see how time after time, when presented with a challenge or a searching question, Jesus responded in terms of the total situation. His reply was directed not merely to the argument, but to the underlying motive, and was specially relevant to the human situation.

Because the response of Jesus was to total situations, his statements can only be properly understood in the light of those situations. If we fail to recognize the nature of the situations his statements will often seem contradictory, as in the instance I have already mentioned, the statements concerning the Law. At

* C. J. Cadoux, in *The Life of Jesus* (Penguin) makes the same point and further explains that "the Aramaic which Jesus spoke would probably contain no word actually corresponding to the Greek for 'is'".

times he behaved as though the Law were of little importance, and in his statement that the Sabbath was made for man, not man for the Sabbath, he put not merely one rule but the whole Law into a position of secondary importance.* Yet at another time he said that not one jot or tittle shall pass from the Law until all be fulfilled—a statement which if taken literally would mean that Jesus condoned cruelty and the killing of witches—for the Law contained these as well as social wisdom and good hygiene.† We must remember that he was talking at a particular time in history to particular audiences, audiences that varied from day to day, perhaps from home to home. He was not talking to posterity or making ex cathedra judgments to humanity in general. He was right in the middle of a deadly conflict, dogged by men who were determined to get rid of him and his blasphemous, dangerous teaching.

This is not to say that the statements of Jesus are not filled with eternal truth. Of course they are; but we shall miss the nature of the truth if we think that it is simply contained in the literal statements. Jesus' statements are not just words of wisdom; they are the

* Much more could be said about this. In Mark 7, probably very reliable, Jesus definitely sets aside an Old Testament Law (about unclean meats), and distinguishes between tradition and the law of God, between observances and what comes from the heart. The "jot or tittle" statement appears in different contexts in Luke and Matthew. In Luke it comes before an attack on the callous putting away of wives —and this would support my contention about the "total situation". The use of it by Matthew—writing later than Luke—may be part of his general effort to convince the Jewish people, for whom his gospel was specifically written, of the continuity of Jewish tradition and inspiration in Jesus. Statements appearing in Luke and Matthew, but not in Mark, are often considered as coming from a missing document "Q", to which these later writers had access.

† Exodus 22.18. *Thou shalt not suffer a witch to live.*

record that remains to us of what were essentially *actions*; what Jesus *did* when people attacked him or needed him. They indicate how he *responded*. His whole personality and an awareness of the whole situation lay behind the words and conditioned them. We must recreate the situation for ourselves in imagination in order to know what the words meant.

To give an instance, it seems to me quite wrong to lift Jesus' statements about marriage and divorce out of their living context and apply them without imagination or compassion to present-day situations. Jesus was talking to men who were taking advantage of the inferior legal position occupied by women, who were making unscrupulous use of a special dispensation by Moses,* ("because of the hardness of your hearts") to get tired of their wives and then get rid of them.

We must not expect to go to the Gospels for precise directions; that is to belittle Jesus to the status of a schoolmaster. We must rather look to him for an understanding of how the divine perception can penetrate below all appearances to meet real needs. To be like Jesus involves no copy-book exercises; it is not a matter of acquiring virtue and eliminating faults, of obeying rules and following directions; it is a matter of entering imaginatively and deeply into his life so that we can meet the world as he met it; so that we can learn from experience as he did; so that we know how to meet the many situations that are not described even in the Gospels. It is in the unexpected that our inner quality is tested.

There is one story told of Jesus that appears only in

* Deuteronomy 24, 1-2. A dispensation of which unlimited advantage could be taken.

John's Gospel, so that its authenticity may be a little in doubt—the story of the woman taken in adultery. But it is so convincing an example of what I have been describing that I find it almost impossible to believe that it did not happen. The woman is caught *in flagrante delicto* and hauled before Jesus. Now we'll test him! See what he makes of this! The unimaginative, safe response would have been to lecture on her immorality and then beg her captors to exercise mercy. But no, Jesus did not do that. He paused and doodled in the sand, giving himself time to see right through to the heart of the situation—to perceive that it was the men's cruelty and hypocrisy, not the woman's adultery, that was the truly shocking and horrible fact. Then he gave that dramatic and unanswerable response, "Let him who is without sin amongst you cast the first stone." And when he was at last left alone with her he did not condemn. He had saved her from being stoned to death and he gently asked her not to sin again.

Most of us can claim that we have escaped from the Sunday-School conception of Jesus, the immaculate white-robed figure. But I doubt whether any of us have yet fully outgrown the false background that was provided for that unreal figure—the gentle sunlit country side, the charming romantic figures of Palestinian children, women with water pots and bearded men in cloak and burnous. You can this very day stand on the mound that covers the ancient city of Jericho and watch the women coming to Elisha's well, dressed just as in the Biblical illustrations. You can look to the right down the green strip of the Jordan valley drenched in sunshine and see it in the stage setting for the Gentle Teacher. But look to the left and you see that the women are coming from a great densely crowded mass of tiny huts, where thousands of Arab refugees from Israel live miserably and hopelessly on United Nations charity, proud and bitter. Under the sea of tiny roofs lives a large proportion of the half million refugees in Jordan, the continuing tragedy of one of the world's "irreducible dilemmas". If that is the kind of truth we must recognize in Palestine today—a situation full of evil and danger—how much more keenly we should be aware of it in the Palestine of Jesus's time! We cannot see him truly unless we see him moving about in a community seething with hatreds and torn with bitter conflicts.* It was not only a matter of Jew against Roman, but Jew against Jew. Judea was an occupied country and "collaborators" were many. From the very district whence Jesus came there were organized groups of men pledged to their assassination. Suicidal fanaticism, treachery, fratricide and infanticide were common experiences. How absurd it is in view of this to think of the statements of Jesus as though they were made to a congregation of Anglican bishops or a group of Quaker social workers.

* See Cecil Roth: *Short History of the Jewish People* (East & West Library) Chap. IX also Josephus: *The Jewish War* (Penguin).

VI

RELIGION IN FETTERS

WE have seen how Jesus used the imaginative approach to understand what God wanted of him and to understand and meet the needs of people. If he needed imagination then so do we, to understand him and to enable us to enter his way of life. Can it be said that organized Christianity encourages the use of imagination?

In recent years, among Biblical scholars, the imagination has been brilliantly at work. The scientific study of the Biblical documents, like all scientific work, has required imagination for the sorting out and piecing together of fragments until a convincing picture emerges. The scholars who undertook this work had to be free in mind, free from the demands of any authority but that of truth itself and the integrity of their approach, free from the fear that dispassionate study could destroy the foundation of faith. The picture that emerges is convincing, far more convincing than the unenlightened approach to the Gospels could ever have been.

I would illustrate this by one example. W. R. Maltby* shows how immeasurably our understanding of the story of the Temptations has become deepened by seeing it in its historical, personal and documentary setting. As he says, "None of the older commentators has anything to say that is worth consulting on that

* *The Significance of Jesus* (S.C.M. Press 1948).

episode. They did not apprehend its meaning . . . The Temptation falls to the level of a sham fight between an omniscient God and a not very subtle devil. It is pathetic that men intellectually so endowed . . . should have visited that desert scene blindfold and left nothing behind but a litter of tracts."

Taken as it stands the temptation story has the quality of legend rather than of fact. It must therefore be understood imaginatively. What is recorded must have come from the mouth of Jesus alone; there could have been no spectators. What we read must be only a brief residue of what he said to his friends when he returned to them, and it is cast in the thought forms, the poetry and imagery of his time. It is unreasonable to expect Jesus to have talked in the phraseology of an age to which he did not belong, but it is equally un-reasonable to use his report as though it required no translation into the language of our own day. Seen with the help of all that scholarship can bring to it, the event was an intense focus to which Jesus brought the whole history and tradition of his people, his con-sciousness of God tremendously at work in that history, his awareness of the powerful forces urging him to take this course or that—forces operating not only in his community but in conflict within himself.

Thinking along these lines, what do we make of the temptation to throw himself down? Could he have had in mind the eschatological material of the Book of Daniel,* in which God is described as appearing in the clouds or descending from Heaven?—material that had much significance for the Jews during the wars of the Maccabees. Jesus's mind was well stocked with

* Daniel 7, 14-15.

54

his nation's sacred writings; perhaps one phrase or another occurred to him, taken from the Psalms or Deuteronomy. As he meditated on the way in which he might make God known to man, first one and then another course suggested by these sacred books would be weighed in his mind. Not all was of equal value; the ecstatic promise from Psalm 91 that angels would bear him up as he floated down to men's view from the Temple towers gave way to the cool steadiness of the Deuteronomic voice that said one must not put God to the test. So clear in his mind is the relative value of the two sayings that the voice from the Psalms is put into the mouth of the Devil.

The result of the scientific and scholarly investigation of Biblical documents is, however, known only to a small fraction of Christian believers. Looking over the whole Christian Church one can fairly say that the great majority of worshippers are dependent on ritual, symbolism and doctrine that continue unmodified through the centuries, yet implying—some of it— outmoded views; and on preaching that is uninformed by the knowledge that scholarship has made possible. In general it is still true to say that people's knowledge of the Gospels is unsupported by an awareness of how and when they were put together and of the historical background and inheritance of Jesus.

Is it not true to say that while civilization, society and secular knowledge are changing with ever-accelerated speed, the way the Christian Church attempts to pass on its truths to the great mass of worshippers remains largely unchanged? Does it not need a new freedom if it is to keep pace with needs? Some of those deeply concerned with the eternal truths may think this suggestion indicates the conditioned approach of one who is a "child of his age"; but as I see it there is a sharp and disturbing contrast between the freedom that science enjoys and the bondage in which religious expression remains. It is true that there is a big difference between the objective, separable, rapidly developing interests of science and the unchanging problems of the human spirit. But, feeling as I am for a unity in all human activity, I think it right to suggest that in science and religion the setting free of thought and imagination is equally necessary.

It is a prevalent attitude among religious people to think of religion and the Christian faith as the last defence against the rapidly assembling forces of destruction in the modern world; they tend to *fall back* upon their faith, tensing their spiritual muscles, surveying their resources as though their supplies were running out. But there is another way of living that may encourage a very different perception of our resources. Suppose that it is God's intention, not that we shall be defeated but that what we want to happen will happen. Suppose that our fears of destruction are lifted and we see perhaps thousands of years of creative development stretching ahead of mankind. Dare we look forward to what religion might become if it ceased to be on the defensive? When we are frightened —and religion is, alas, shot through with fear and distaste of the world—we tend to look backward to what we once had, or think we had. But what if we stop being afraid?

Let me emphasize that this is indeed an intensely creative world that we are living in. It is an exciting, exhilarating world to be born into, in which new possibilities are ever opening up to mankind: possibilities of physical exploration and of human communication, understanding and enjoyment. The rapidity of change, so accelerated by scientific activity, frightens us all at times. But that is no reason to deplore it; we must accept it, we must even enjoy it. It is not enough to take our stand on an ancient culture and try to appear benevolent and hopeful spectators; we must be right in the main current of activity, understanding and directing it.

If we take, if only for a moment, this more confident view of the human future, can we assume that ritual, doctrine and religious phraseology will remain unchanged forever? Considering this we at once think of the changelessness of Christ, and perhaps we link this up with the thought of other great people, how their personality speaks unchanged across the centuries. But is it not an absurdity to believe that the truth about them will forever continue to be expressed in the same words, that ritual that was meaningful to the first few centuries after Christ will still be wholly appropriate and adequate to the life of people in A.D. 3000? Will the new wine continue for ever to be poured into old bottles?

It should be recognized that much of what is thought to be essential to Christianity, and therefore to be permanent in it, does not derive from the Gospels but from the centuries that followed, from the activities of the fifth century that resulted in the creeds, from mediaeval scholasticism, the struggles of the Reformation, from Puritans and from evangelical revivals. This mass of statement and doctrine may contain elements of eternal significance, but it also reflects the peculiar needs and habits of thought of the historical period concerned. These needs and habits do not coincide with those of today. Science is profoundly changing our way of approach to problems. Even those who are not scientists cannot avoid the impact of science upon their minds. If we are to be in the modern world and inevitably affected by it, and if at the same time our thinking about religion and our statement of its truths are to be cast in a mediaeval mould, the result must be a split mind, what Koestler, describing the beginnings of the split in the seventeenth century, calls the "controlled schizophrenia" of the age.

There are many people who can still pour the wine of the spirit into the silver chalice of the Communion, but looked at in the perspective of time they are a decreasing number. It seems true that greatly increased numbers of people in the United States attend places of worship, but none of the descriptions of the attitudes involved suggests a new spiritual sensitiveness. It is also true that the Catholic Church in this country is increasing its membership, but I see no sign that its members are better able to address themselves to the problems of this age. It involves no disparagement of one's Catholic friends to say that Catholicism seems to ask from the rank and file a simple-minded credulity that is incompatible with the world of science into whose activities that very rank and file are being swept.

Although Friends have put aside ritual in their own worship, they do not deplore it or even criticize it in those larger sections of the Christian Church where it is still used. There may be many Friends who, while they have no desire for it themselves, will be a little shocked at the suggestion that Christian ritual and symbolism might change. Looking into oneself for the origin of this suggestion it seems to be more in feeling, in a "hunch", than in logical judgment. This feeling is at its strongest where the extremes of ritual are practised. To watch the Ethiopian Epiphany ceremony —Timcat—in Addis Ababa, is to watch perhaps the most colourful religious ceremony in the world; but delightful as the experience is, one is left with the feeling that it has nothing to do with daily life; indeed, Ethiopian monophysite Christianity seems to have practically no implications for human behaviour. But also to wander from church to church in Athens during Easter or to watch the torchlight procession in Siena, is to get much the same impression—that people are, in these observances, stepping out of the present into the past, a past that is not without a dark barbaric element. In what way does it nourish them; is the world of today any better for what appears to be a sort of split-consciousness? I find it difficult to believe that as the organization and mode of thought of the daily world move on with their present pace, this dipping into the past can remain, even as much as it is now, related to secular experience and conduct.

In Britain religious ceremony has much more austerity, but it does not differ in kind, and *if* criticism of the extreme is justified it must have some relevance to the less extreme. We must clearly face the question— even if the ultimate answer is to be *no*—as to whether the past is in any way holding us in bondage.

There will be some readers with a knowledge of psychology and anthropology, conversant with the classification of figures and symbols and powers into archetypes, who would urge that because they are archetypal they will remain unchanged in significance. To this I would reply that there is no reason why man should remain dominated by his archetypal entities in a particular mode of expression, and that progress towards maturity involves a measure of control and modification of their operation. There has been a wide variation over different epochs and cultures.

It might also be argued that just as great art is eternal in its significance, so the medium of worship—which is akin to art—should remain unchanged and will continue to meet the deepest and unchanging needs in man. But great works of art are not only eternal; in another aspect they are "dated"—indissolubly related to their period. We are made immediately aware of this when a historian gives us the complete historical setting of a picture and it then becomes brilliantly alive. It would be outrageous to expect a young artist today to paint in the manner of Rembrandt or Fra Angelico, even though he humbly accepted them as Immortals. It is not in form but in living relationship—a kind of action—that the eternal quality exists, and this applies to art, poetry, ethics, and philosophy, which from the other point of view can be just as much dated as science. To me this view is parallel with the concept of God not as an eternal Idea or collection of ideas but as Creator, living and loving, eternally significant *in his activity*.

It must be remarked that to suggest that religious ritual and symbolism might change and develop is not to imply that existing ritual is necessarily useless or insincere or that it fails to enrich and deepen the lives of particular individuals. This would be as foolish as to say that because a modern artist must find his own sincere expression he cannot be deeply moved by the fifteenth-century Fra Angelico in Florence.

A Quaker who finds it difficult to appreciate religious ritual and symbolism is not fitted even to suggest ways in which the form of worship associated with them might change. His job is rather to look at his own religious community with a critical eye. Moreover the problem is how to find a release, for without that the production of new forms is impossible. We cannot think new thoughts until we are free to do so. This is illustrated by my own problem in painting pictures— the almost insuperable difficulty of setting myself free from traditional and imposed ways of seeing and interpreting; until I can overcome this I cannot see freshly and clearly nor paint with a vision and sincerity that are my own.

Though Friends have rejected the dramatic and colourful forms of ritual, they have not escaped ritual behaviour. They may reject the idea that the body of Christ is present in the wafer, but they accept with full ritualistic rigidity that God ceases to have any message for them promptly at 12 o'clock on Sunday morning and that the meeting must therefore be closed on the hour. Our silence can at times become an oppressive ritual; the Inner Light, too consciously thought about, withdraws and fails to illumine; and our straining, often with tired minds, to drive away casual thoughts, produces only inhibition. The Quaker method of worship, receiving no help from symbol or physical activity, requires both freshness and relaxation if it is to be successful. We speak of "centring down" with such gravity that in the effort to achieve it we sometimes find ourselves groping in a bottomless pit. We should ask ourselves if worship should always be solemn, if there ought not to be room for spontaneity and even laughter. And must ministry always be a statement of faith or a conclusion; why not the posing of a simple question?

It is in relation to the use of words that criticism is as applicable to the Society of Friends as to any other Christian body, and it is perhaps specially important in that, in the absence of symbols, words are our sole means of communication and expression. One cannot ask for great precision in the use of words, for this would be to ask for an intellectual training which only the few can have. Further, sincerity and imagination can shine through even a fumbling use of words. The enemy we have to fight is the cliché and the sanctified word or phrase.

Any good teacher of English is severely critical of the use of clichés by his pupils—conventional over-worked phrases that are used to indicate an attitude, a kind of situation, a feeling. His reason is that they tend to substitute second-hand feeling for first-hand personal experience; they do not stimulate the writer to discover what his own feelings really are, but offer a ready-made and lazy alternative. If a boy writes that the airplane zoomed across the sky you have no evidence that he has listened attentively to it, but if he writes that it made a sound like tearing calico it suggests that he really has and that in the very act of searching for words and exercising his imagination, he discovered more about the sound. In searching for words to describe our feelings we deepen those feelings.

Why is it that in teaching English we deplore clichés but in religious speech we exalt them? Even such phrases as the Grace of God, the love of God, the suffering of our Lord, redeeming power, atonement, can become clichés, not only losing their original significance but destroying our ability to think and feel sincerely. Far from being recognized as second-hand and overworked, these phrases are thought of as precious and hallowed by usage. This is the point where religious expression goes seriously wrong.

Of all religious clichés the very worst is the word *sin*. I know that literally it means only missing the mark, but it is used with the implication of moral delin-quency and it lumps together a great mass of actions many of which have nothing in common with the rest. There is something that I would still wish to be called sinful—a deliberate turning of one's back on what is known to be good—"evil be thou my good"—but beyond this I see this overworked word sin as a definite stumbling block in the way of understanding and redirection of human behaviour. In one's attempts to gain the sympathy of the thoughtful atheist or agnostic, it is a sheer nuisance. To the deeply sensitive and humble person, seeing himself in the light of the generosity and love of God, all his deficiencies are a missing of the mark; he cannot let himself get away with anything. For him "sin" can continue to have a deeply significant and wholesome meaning. But so it is with all clichés; in origin and to the initiated they can have the greatest significance. But to the outsider, and to the fumbling, the accusation of sin is—just a blow in the face. How well Jesus knew that!

I would not have religion divest its language of such

words as redemption and Incarnation, but I would
have it cease to use such words with the facility that
implies that their meaning is obvious. Whenever there
is occasion to use them, the preacher or writer should
make an effort to use other words in order to be sure
that he is not just passing on a vague emotion or
becoming content with an accepted meaning.

If I switch on the radio in the middle of a broadcast
sermon, I sometimes experience an almost overwhelming sense of the decline and death of Christianity
—a feeling from which it takes me some time to recover.
Phrase follows phrase with a dull inevitability; words
that were once full of life now empty of meaning,
rolling off a tongue too well trained; feelings that were
once real and spontaneous now mere conventional
sentiments. In the very act of making these phrases
precious we attach feeling to the words instead of to
the experience they attempt to represent. Phrases
treated in this way gather round them a detached
emotion of their own, an autonomous power, and thus
they become a danger to clear thinking and sincere
feeling. We must search and search again for new
words, new phrases to describe and explore our religious
experience—otherwise our religion will not remain
alive and our experience will become a staged per-
formance.

A critic might wish to make the point that in any
department of thought there is a need for terms that
have a generally agreed meaning, to facilitate discussion and communication. But the difficulty about
so many religious terms is that even if they have a
generally agreed meaning to theological specialists,
they are used to and by the ordinary worshipper as

emotive words and phrases not adequately linked to experience. Scientific terms cannot be used in this way because their meaning is all the time being checked by what happens on the bench or in the test-tube. Scientists can mutilate English and produce "jargon" but always there is a compulsion towards precision and development of meaning.

Admittedly there is a difference between the terminology of religion and science, in that religious experience is a matter of deep personal feeling, for which exact and adequate expression is impossible. It would therefore be ridiculous to plead for exactness in the semantic or scientific sense. To explain what is necessary I must refer back to what I have said about poetry, in which words are used emotively and yet with precision—and to enrich our knowledge. We need more than discussion; we need discovery, and therefore we must never be content with habitual phrases or agreed meanings.

Together with the encouragement of clichés, religious groups tend to destroy imagination and to inhibit genuine experience by dictating what might be called appropriate emotional attitudes. If we try to condition young people towards reverence, humility, adoration, we shall obtain all too often a counterfeit. Deep and sincere feeling is not at all easy for children to experience in the world as it is. They are exposed to numerous influences tending to provide them with conventional emotions, so that they derive a standardized and often false conception of what is beautiful, admirable, worth emulating. In religious thought we may believe that our conceptions are more certain, more discriminating, but if we present them in the same way as the world we criticize presents its values, they will have little more significance; they will be inadequate to deal with the unexpected experience.

Even the feelings which we believe to be the very source of our religious understanding and faith can be hollow—precisely because they are feelings that are trained into us, feelings that we have been made to feel we ought to have. This is well illustrated in the Epilogue to Shaw's *St. Joan* when the ghosts of Cauchon and de Stogumber are discussing the death of Joan.

> *Cauchon:* Were not the sufferings of our Lord Christ enough for you?
>
> *de Stogumber:* No. Oh no; not at all. I had seen them in pictures and read of them in books, and been greatly moved by them, as I thought. But it was no use: it was not our Lord that redeemed me, but a young woman whom I actually saw burned to death. It was dreadful, oh most dreadful. But it saved me. I have been a different man ever since, though a little astray in my wits sometimes.
>
> *Cauchon:* Must then a Christ perish in torment in every age to save those who have no imagination?

Another force in organized Christianity inimical to imagination is the legislative and administrative mind, the attitude that seeks primarily to control behaviour and to tidy up the otherwise wayward and unpredictable conduct of human beings by laws, rules, codes and rigid morals. Jesus found himself severely in conflict with this force in his own community. The Jewish urge towards righteousness and awareness of wrongdoing had hardened into a concept of sin, elaborated by the priestly legislators into a pattern so fierce and rigid that it was impossible for a man or woman to live an ordinary life without a consciousness of continual sin, and right conduct had become a stereotyped pattern of trivial observances. Time and time again Jesus was compelled to break through this in order to show what fulfilment of the deeper Law really meant. It is a commentary on human weakness and perversity that within so short a time of Jesus' death the Church was at work creating an elaborate hierarchy of sins and penetrating into the most intimate details of a man's daily life with judgments implying delinquency and guilt. This persists right into the present day, for you can read a modern book published for the guidance of millions of worshippers, which discusses at length in what circumstances a kiss is or is not a mortal sin (it would appear that only the most passionless peck is permissible before marriage!) and continues in the same vein about the sensations a boy feels when he slides down the bannister rail. In one aspect this is humorous; but in another one is driven to anger and almost despair at the thought of how the loving generous passionate message of Jesus has been reduced to this mean-minded niggling.

It is true that the Church could offer—as the Scribes and Pharisees could not—a concept of forgiveness and redemption, but this put all the more power into the hands of the law makers, administrators and power-seekers. If you can convince a man of sin and at the same time persuade him that your Church can bring forgiveness that will lift his guilt, then you have him wholly in your power. There is no doubt that this situation was exploited by those whose temperaments were those of legislators.

The Church, for all its claims to divine guidance,

is a human institution and has shown the contradiction and paradox always present in human institutions. It has lived in unceasing tension between the urge to discipline and dominate the Christian community and the impulse to reach intimacy with God, an experience that takes a man beyond rules to the point where he can say with St. Augustine: "Love God and do what you like." Thus its greatest saints have walked on a razor edge between orthodoxy and arch-heresy.

It is saddening to recognize how the Church in its organization rapidly and thoroughly took over most of those attributes of the Scribes and Pharisees that Jesus so fiercely condemned. However broadly doctrine might be interpreted, practice and rule sought to imprison God within the organization, and the wind of the spirit, which for Jesus "bloweth where it listeth", could be felt only in ecclesiastical precincts. One result has been that even today many believers, and even half-believers, cannot imagine God working outside the organization that the Church has provided for him. In practice they severely limit the omnipotence they accord to God in theory. Recent controversies about the re-marriage of divorced persons have shown this poverty of imagination in a startling way. Two people acting hurriedly, cynically, thoughtlessly, or even under evil coercion, can have their marriage solemnized in church. It seems that to many people not only are the two young people trapped into a relationship which they cannot make real, but God also is trapped into blessing what may be wicked. This is not Christianity but a survival of the evil magic of the witch-doctor.

The pattern of sin—guilt—forgiveness, so easily tending to become the dead residue of a living experience, can be as limiting to the human spirit as any other pattern taken over and made a matter of organization. Moreover it was much easier to create an overwhelming burden of guilt than to make the love of God evident through an imperfect Church and priesthood. The result in the time of the Desert Fathers was to drive sensitive souls almost to insanity. It is a tribute to the positive truth and underlying vigour of Christianity that some saints rose to such heights of perception in spite of a burden of suffering and self-torture that was surely unnecessary.

The focus of guilt in their time, perhaps always, was the sexual impulse. It is only in recent times that we have begun to escape from the assumption that all sexual impulse is a guilty thing unfortunately necessary for procreation. But we have moved far enough to be able to look back upon the attitudes of the Dark Ages with incredulous horror and disgust. How can we assess a burden of guilt so great that self-castration was a relatively common occurrence and that the greatest of the Early Fathers—Origen—was driven to it? St. Augustine devotes a chapter to the expression of his wish that all desire should be taken from procreation, and that a man should move his genitals by as cold an act of will as he ordinarily moves his hands or legs. Aquinas thought it unwise for near relatives to marry*—not for biological reasons, but because they might be so close as to be fond of each other and thus too much moved by passion. This was his reason for the ban on incest.

* *Contra Gentiles* iii. 125. For an interesting discussion of this point in particular and of love in the medieval setting see C. S. Lewis: *The Allegory of Love* (Oxford University Press, 1936).

Associated with this guilt went a hatred of the body and a distaste for life; these were expressed in the most appalling self-inflicted tortures, in a repudiation of cleanliness, a wallowing in dirt and a fanatical impulse to martyrdom.*

How did this canker enter Christianity? It is not easy to give a complete answer. The world of the fifth century reflected the degeneracy and perversions of the crumbling Roman civilization; it was dirty, insanitary and disease-ridden. For the people of that time there was no prospect of a deliverance from these conditions, for although modern science can be regarded as in part the product of the Christian impulse to rise above and to control matter, its early developments came too slowly to offer any perceptible hope. So to people who were unusually sensitive, sexual love seemed inseparable from lust and dirt, and the body deserved punishment for its apparent denial of the purity of love.† This can be only a partial answer; the tentative beginnings of a repudiation of sex are to be found at a much earlier stage—in the writings of Paul.

However it is not my task to investigate origins. What I want to point out is that we still suffer from an inheritance of fear and guilt left to us by this period of monstrous spiritual and physical perversion. The Catholic Church has never fully shaken off this inheritance. It still condemns as mortal sins experiences that for most children are unavoidable in the process of

---

* See Lecky: *History of European Morals* (Watts, 1946).

† J. Wren-Lewis in a remarkable and enlightening broadcast ("A Vindication of Romance." *The Listener*, October 1st, 1959) gave a similar reason for the attraction to the Gnostic heresy. It was intolerable to many people in that insanitary world to imagine Jesus born as other babies were born. There is a further reference to this broadcast on p. 83.

growing up, ignoring psychiatric evidence. It condemns —at least in its official attitude—any sexual experience outside the conventional code, irrespective of whether it is an expression of the greatest generosity and tenderness or is an expression of sheer lust. Protestantism has been as deeply affected as Catholicism, and when fear of sex in the form of Puritanism has taken charge there has been no escape whatever for the guilty one.

We can perhaps understand what William Blake felt when he wrote in *The Marriage of Heaven and Hell:*

> As the caterpillar chooses the fairest leaves to lay her
> eggs on,
> so the priest lays his curse on the fairest joys.

It is here that Quakerism enters the picture, for there is an element of Puritanism in Quakerism that makes it difficult for some Friends to understand people who are less obviously "spiritual" in their habits. Among Friends the emphasis has perhaps changed; instead of a rigid concept of sin there is sometimes a rigid concept of integrity, which can produce an insuperable barrier between those who live according to a pattern of goodness and those who do not.

I do not subscribe to the view that all the disorders and failures of mankind arise from sexual indulgence or frustration, but it is obvious that a very great deal of unhappiness has a sexual origin, and anything we can do to reach a better understanding we must not fail to do. This will require a freeing of ourselves from the taboos, fears and cruel judgments of the past. It is impossible to reach the roots of human conduct, to make possible the growth of loving relationships and the flowering of the abundant life, if we insist on putting actions into categories, classifying them in their superficial resemblances as right or wrong. Christianity requires that we shall feel compassion for the sufferer. This does not mean merely feeling sorry for him—for we can feel that without any understanding. No, compassion means entering imaginatively and deeply into the life of the sufferer, recognizing the whole network of forces in which he is caught, and we cannot do this if our minds are dominated by a respect for rules and codes and taboos. Jesus had respect for law and for community standards, but his first impulse was always to reach the sufferer; and law, custom and morality had to stand aside until this intimacy was achieved.

VII

THE NEED FOR HUMILITY

I HAVE made clear my opinion—and I do not put it forward as anything but a personal opinion—that the Christian Church has at times in its history been profoundly mistaken. If to sin is to "miss the mark" then not only have individual Christians sinned but so has the Church itself, sinned grievously and time after time. It has fostered a misapprehension of what Jesus sought to do, and incorporated attitudes that, far from being really Christian, were condemned by Jesus himself. When I try to defend Christianity against the arguments of the atheist or agnostic, I still have to meet the charge that organized Christianity, Catholic and Protestant, has been responsible for an immeasurable amount of suffering—for wars, persecution, torture, every kind of cruelty and intolerance. This is a stale argument, but one cannot deny its truth. We have been shocked at the intensely concentrated inhumanity and cruelty of the Nazi regime,* but the people who suffered were

* Even for this, Christians and their Church cannot disclaim responsibility. The following passage appeared in an outspoken leader in the *Observer* at Christmas time 1959:

"One of the most fantastic stories of history is how Christianity, which started as a sect of Judaism, specially dedicated to mercy rather than justice, gave its moral authority for a thousand years to a merciless hatred of defenceless Jews. It is a measure of human treachery that the Christian Churches have some part of the historic blame for the worst crime that has ever been committed: the systematic destruction of millions of Jewish men and women in Europe in our lifetime. That huge

73   6B

not more in number than those who—spread over a much longer period of time—were tortured, butchered and burnt in the name of Christ. It is not enough to say that these wickednesses were due to the weakness of the individual man. The Church—or those who claim to represent it—must be held responsible too. The Church has been profoundly ambivalent and nowhere has the evil of the split mind been more apparent.

It has sought for, and wielded, tremendous power over the individual and, so it seems to me, has been guilty of the cardinal sin of pride. It has often puzzled me to note the contradiction in some of the most faithful sons of the Church; what appears to be a deep and lovable personal humility in an individual can coexist with an inflexible belief in the rightness of the attitudes and doctrines of his Church—whichever it might be. Often the Church itself in its collective aspect —as an institution responsible for statements—seems to embody a contradiction of what it requires of its members. One would expect that individual humility would produce a collective humility, but it seldom does. It would seem that man—in general—cannot bear to live without certainty. If he is to give up his individual pride he must sink himself in an organization that takes over the arrogance and certainty that he himself gives up. Needless to say, this goes for Marxists as well as for Christians, but in Christianity it is more apparent

---

act of murder could never have been carried out had Christians not for centuries previously suspected, mocked and tormented Jews.

There is nothing peculiar to Christians or Europeans in their cruelty and perversity. Nearly all the religions of the world have been used as a screen for doing the opposite of what those religions have taught. Man has always shown an infinite capacity for self-deception."

as a contradiction of the faith itself. The individual is expected and exhorted to prostrate himself in humility, to admit his ignorance, his poverty of understanding, his inherent sinfulness. But how often have Christian churches or sects, in their corporate life and organization, been ready to confess to an inadequate and confused perception of the will of God, to admit to having sinned, to having led their people astray, to having subordinated spiritual aims to political ends, and obstructed God's purpose? It seems that almost always they have been dogmatic, intransigent, too appallingly right and sometimes guilty of an intolerance not less than that of the Nazis or Communists.

Is it not time that we recognized what a precarious hold we all have on religious truth, how dim is our perception of the will of God, both as individuals and as churches? Can we—all sections of the Christian community—go on making the kind of assertions we do about our hold on truth and expect ever to know what truth *is*? There is something to be said for strong convictions, but they should be convictions as to the way truth is to be found, not convictions as to the possession of it, convictions as to the *need* for God, not convictions as to the statement of his truth.

Scientists, both individually and collectively, have accepted the discipline of humility in their researches. Four hundred years ago they began to break away from the intellectual arrogance and snobbery that was the legacy of Platonism, and to learn that truth was to be found in experience, not by withdrawal into a noumenal world. This is not say that scientists as *men* are humble people, but that their work and their success as scientists depends on their recognizing that they cannot achieve anything unless they first admit that they *do not know*, that they are ignorant.

Religious institutions have tended to proceed in the opposite way. Deeply infected with Platonism the Church has too often said or implied: We have the truth, come in and we will give it you. We have had special access; we are in the know; we are infallible.

The scientist is prepared to be taught progressively by experience. If he makes any assumptions, they are open to the most critical examination. It is often said that a scientist works by faith—faith in the order and rationality of the universe. But this is not the same as an act of faith in the religious sense. To work on the assumption of the orderliness of the universe requires no deliberate intention—for the scientist simply cannot do otherwise; it is in the nature of his situation that he should do so. Scientists as a group can be guilty of arrogance and pride, especially when they work together in large groups without adequate contact with workers in other activities. But there is no central organization to focus and intensify their pride or to take over the certainty they abandon.

How far is Quakerism guilty of the faults I have criticized in the larger body of the Church? At a first glance there seems little collective pride—little pride in possession of ultimate truth or dogma. Where there is any pride it takes the form of a smugness, resulting from the good works the Society has performed and the high standard of morality it has maintained in its members. We fall into the error of people who are too good, who are not at home among publicans and sinners.

It was put to me by a Dominican friend (with the

adroitness one would expect from a member of his Order) that the existence of the Catholic Church is independent of the morality of its adherents; it continues to exist whatever they do, whereas the very existence of the Protestant Church depends upon the morality of its members. In fairness he admitted the corollary that the moral standard of Protestants is higher than that of Catholics, but claimed with glee that the Catholic Church is inclusive, the Protestant exclusive.

One does not have to think long to recognize the evils that can result from a concept of church "existence" that is independent of the way people in it behave; it makes possible an intolerable divorce between precept and practice and a cynical misuse of the Church's provision for dealing with sin. It explains a great deal of the evil in the history of Christianity. But the thought that we* are exclusive through our very standard of morality, is, and should be, a shock. The Society of Friends is highly respected for the "goodness" of its members, but does the obvious sinner find a welcome among us? (I say obvious sinner because our very righteousness may be a hidden sin). Do we make it too difficult for the one to join the ninety-and-nine? The Society of Friends has shown deep and practical compassion for the *sufferer*, but what about the *malefactor*, the one who has chosen the way of cruelty and dishonesty, who knows he has made himself an outcast? What do we do to make our own religious community a place of invitation and restoration?

---

* I am including the Society of Friends among the Protestant churches for this purpose, though strictly it claims not to be Protestant but to be "primitive Christianity revived".

I think my Dominican friend would agree with me that no church really depends upon a standard of morality. If a church has reality it derives it from a recognition and experience of the love of God, of this love at work in the everyday lives of men and women. This experience brings a sense of well-being, of meaning and joy to life. It brought the intensity of revelation and hope to the first Christian communities.

In its organization, its principles and method, Quakerism has, however, almost unlimited possibilities in the modern world. No one who is in touch with both science and Quakerism can fail to see the features they have in common. Like the scientist, we do not start with dogma or articles of faith. We begin with a desire for truth, a commitment to the search for it, and a concept of the disciplined method by which it is to be discovered. We do not expect anything to come to us magically or by any ritualized process—only through a conscious deliberate search. We know that as individuals we have no adequate check upon the development of mere notions within our minds; and so we insist upon the discipline of the worshipping community in which mere waywardness of mind or individualism will be seen for what it is. And we know that the stimulus and personal interchange of the religious community will enable the individual to rise to a greater clarity of perception than would be possible for him alone. We are—at least in theory—committed to no forms of speech, no particular phraseology; we can make our own to fit our experience, to be meaningful in our present day environment.

Quakerism is, potentially, in line with the modern world and its needs. Granted the validity of religious experience, no other form of Christian worship and discipline is better adjusted to the modern world, more unfettered, more capable of creative growth. I can move from laboratory to Meeting for Worship and back without any adjustment of feeling or approach. There is nothing in the one that I have to abjure in the other. Further, the Friends' Meeting—though definitely an expression of a Christian perception—can be the meeting place of people of all persuasions, Christian or otherwise, and the method and attitude of a Friend do not prevent him from participating in the worship of any other Christian community.

At every point, it seems to me, there is a parallel with the inspiration, the freedom, the universality of the world of scientific activity.

Why, then, does the Society of Friends remain the tiny community that it is; why do not the multitudes see in its way the answer to the apparent conflict between science and religion; why, when the Society of Friends has set aside all the apparent reasons for pride and exclusiveness, does it remain in fact so exclusive?

There are many answers to this question and I shall not attempt to find them all. One obvious answer is that Quakerism makes little concession to human weakness. It places a heavy burden of conscience and responsibility upon the individual—too great for most people. Many a writer, looking at the Society of Friends from outside, has observed that we have tried to re-capture the spirit of early Christianity. The nature of our religious community and the distribution of responsibility among its members are characteristic of this attempt. But in early Christianity—and in the early Quakerism of the 17th century—there were also joy and excitement and inspiration that made the humblest member a full participant. We cannot now "manufacture" on a nation-wide scale the religious fervour of early Christianity or of the 17th century, and the humbler worshipper of today therefore finds more attraction, and possibly a more obvious meeting of his needs, where more of the work is done *for* him, and less expected *from* him to begin with.

Friends often enough refer to spiritual joy in their ministry, but it is a pity that there is not more outward expression of it. In proportion to our members we have taken on a very large share of Christian service, but how much have we discovered of what Jesus meant when he said "My yoke is easy and my burden is light."?

We ought to be joyful, not in a mysterious inward sense only, but in a way that everyone can recognize. If we have discovered the water of life we ought to be exuberant; whereas in fact we often seem too serious and apprehensive. It may be that we are still suffering from the legacy of the period in the Society's history when it tragically misunderstood the world of art, and could not distinguish gaiety and exuberance from worldly extravagance and indulgence.

This deprived us of one of the great sources of religious experience and one of its most potent expressions; it has left our imagination dim.

In Art I include imaginative literature and poetry, music, painting, sculpture and drama. In relation to all these, we have now consciously repudiated our mistake but we have not wholly recovered from it. The Society's poverty of output in these activities is in startling contrast to its richness of scientific output. The number of distinguished Quaker novelists, poets, painters and dramatists is negligibly small compared with the number of distinguished scientists.

I must say at once that I should not be reassured merely to find a number of Friends composing modern music, writing modern novels or drama, or contributing paintings to the most modern section of the Tate Gallery. Not all modern art or literature is unifying and exuberant; much of it merely reflects the bewilderment, frustration and fragmentation of our culture. The task of a religious society is to find a way through—to overcome fear and frustration, to bring the fragments of culture together into a new synthesis. How do the arts stand in relation to this? Artistic activity must not be thought of as the deliberate instrument of social change, to be used for that purpose and then set aside; it is an expression of truth, of a sincere relation between the creator and his world, something he must immerse himself in, irrespective of consequences. In this it is not different from what is called pure science and like science it is inevitably an instrument of change, and indispensable. We are nourished by art and poetry, and our constructive task is ill-informed, our vision unclear, and our effectiveness reduced if we deny their part in our lives.

I have already suggested that the creative scientist benefits from a wide experience of other interests and activities through the stimulus and variety that they contribute to his imagination. Equally I would say that in our religious activity we need every kind of experience to enrich our minds, to deepen our contact with life, to prepare us for that movement of the imagination that will take us beyond the present frustration. It is not by intense effort or thought, by heavy seriousness or a deep sense of responsibility that we shall discover the way forward, but by letting in the light, perhaps through hitherto unrecognized windows.

We do need new light, but we also need clearer eyes with which to use it, and I think again of that phrase "liberation from the cataract of accepted beliefs". There is a good deal of fear, confusion and immaturity associated with accepted Christian beliefs. One of the seeming absurdities in the statements of many Christians is the fear of the decline of religion. But if God is a God of love, as we believe him to be, then he cannot desert his world. He cannot treat us as one of his experimental failures to be pitched into the waste-bin of his cosmic laboratory. If it seems to us that God has deserted his world it must be because we have a wrong concept of him, are searching for him in the wrong place or looking for him through the eyes of people long dead. God is either in us and with us or he is a complete illusion.

It is perhaps still true to say that most Christian believers think of an earthly life as preparation for heaven, and may still think of heaven as a place where difficulties and pain will cease, mysteries will be explained and all truth become clearly apparent. The absurdity of such a prospect becomes immediately apparent if we ask how much fun we should get out of science if there were no difficulties in theory or experiment, no demands on our ingenuity; what truth would mean to us if it were presented to us neat and tidy and complete. Christianity is mixed up with

infantile longings and day-dreams, and spiritual reactions that date from a time when the world was a
far more painful, frightening and depressing place to
live in than it is now—a time when there seemed not
only no *prospect* of controlling circumstances, but no
possibility. Disease, terrestrial calamity, war, corruption,
depravity and vice were the inescapable accompani-
ments of human existence. Christianity brought hope
into a dark world, but at first it was hope of a spiritual
deliverance only, and during the first few centuries
of the Christian Church there was little thought or
intention of controlling the environment, except in
pockets of communist experiment; believers simply
awaited, with joy and patience, the Second Coming.
Then, as Wren-Lewis has pointed out:

> The scientific revolution took place in Christendom,
> and nowhere else, precisely because Christendom
> carried at its heart the conviction that nature was
> relative and manipulable.*

He further says:

> I believe that our scientific and technological culture
> is a profoundly Christian culture: more Christian in its
> unconscious assumptions than the so-called ages of
> faith were in their conscious professions. Our great
> need is to make these assumptions more fully conscious,
> to see them in a proper historical perspective, and
> to work out a rational basis for them.*

Our present-day world, in spite of all that we deplore
in it, is a world of immense positive achievement. War
exposed not only man's continued potentiality for evil,
but also his great courage and unending resourcefulness,

* J. Wren-Lewis (Assistant Controller of Research, I.C.I.), *The
Listener*, October 1st, 1959.

and, in extremity, his love for his neighbour. The subsequent period has been overshadowed by the threat of atomic weapons, but it has also illustrated the tremendous resilience of humanity. We are living in an age where there is almost unlimited possibility of direction and control; it is an age profoundly different from the centuries in which the Christian Church was first established. We need a new perception, a different emphasis, to recognize how the eternal truths of our faith remain significant in these altered circumstances.

It is not a world to escape from but a world to accept. It is not only our physical but also our spiritual home, and we should see now that Christianity is not a preparation for, or a means of escape to, a different kind of existence; it is a way of life in a world of conflict. The Kingdom of Heaven intersects at every point with the world of daily experience.

In an immediate and urgent sense the realization of the Kingdom of Heaven implies the unification of the world, the brotherhood of nations—shown to us in terrible clarity by its shocking alternative. That is why our party politics have become less significant than they used to be. The sheer necessity of making that Kingdom come on earth outshines every other consideration. What kingdom in heaven can we hope for if we destroy the hope of the kingdom on earth?

VIII

THE FALSITY OF DUALISM

I HAVE already referred to Platonism as an infection that attacked the Christian Church. This is not to question Plato's greatness or entirely to deplore the union of Christian theology with Greek philosophic thought, but I do suggest that this union has been a very mixed blessing. Plato postulated a dualism—two worlds, one the world of phenomena, of ordinary experience, a world of only passing significance and which moreover *obscured* his other world, which was the world of eternal truth, the noumenal world where truth was self-subsistent, independent of its recognizable manifestations, where, for instance, the truths of triangularity existed independently of any visible or tangible triangles.

It is difficult to believe that Plato did not have his tongue in his cheek when he put into the mouth of Socrates a eulogy of the topmost heights inhabited by the immortals.* For them there was "real existence, colourless, formless and intangible, visible only to the intelligence which sits at the helm of the soul, and with which the family of true science is concerned."† I wonder if Plato ever stood among the spring flowers on the slopes of Parnassus and looked down over

---

* I have been assured the Greek philosophers took themselves seriously; their attitude to their philosophy was not a "professional" one.
† *Phaedrus.*

Delphi and the lovely valley below? And did he really then want to replace that immediate experience—an overwhelming experience for us today—by an intellectual concept of abstract Beauty visible only to the intelligence at the helm of the soul? Yet precisely that attitude to experience is what we find in the dualism that our culture has inherited—yes, profoundly affecting even our grammar school and university education.

Moreover Plato seems quite seriously to have rated poets and artists among his lowest classes, just above farmers and artisans but well below warriors, politicians, merchants, gymnasts and even soothsayers. He denounced art as a sham and a deception. This was the philosophy that was mixed by churchmen with the literature of the most deeply poetic nation of that ancient world!*

The process seems to have begun early in the history of the Church. There is a hint of it in Paul. What did he mean when he said, "When that which is perfect is come, then that which is in part shall be done away . . . For now we see through a glass darkly; but then face to face."? J. B. Phillips' translation runs: "At present all we see is the baffling reflection of reality; we are like men looking at a landscape in a small mirror. The time will come when we shall see reality face to face." It is not impossible that Paul—an educated

---

* This is not to say that the "mediaeval synthesis"—the work of such men as Aquinas—was not a tremendous achievement, but that we should stop being merely respectful, recognize what we have lost in the process, and do something about it.

And in fairness to Plato, it should be added that he was a divided person. In words of Lord Lindsay (whose preface to the Dialogues in the Everyman edition is well worth reading), "He was himself both poet and philosopher, and the quarrel between poetry and philosophy was waged in his own breast."

man—was here under the influence of the Platonic dualism.

Mediaeval churchmen, pathetically attempting to marry the careful logic of the Greeks to the exuberant poetry of the Jews, performed some extraordinary intellectual exercises. It is difficult to believe that the world is any better for many of these antics, though it may be risking the criticism of respected scholars to say so. The consequences run right through into modern religious statement and produce startling contradictions. Father Andrew, in "Meditations for Every Day"—a series of statements that on other pages express much warmth and wisdom—produces this surprising statement on his first page: "The nature of God is wholly other than our own. . . . The life of God in its immense richness and spiritual priority existed before ever He called a creature into being. We are not necessary to God. He is altogether and completely sufficient for himself." This may be interesting as the conclusion of an exercise in mediaeval logic; but it is a thorough-going expression of the dualism, and in relation to our life it has no meaning; it is nonsense. Moreover, it has no support from the Gospels. To Jesus, God was the loving Father, and was there ever a loving father who had no need of his children? This is the kind of contradiction that the "intellectual antics" lead to, and it has done Christianity harm; it has turned attention away from action and relationship, which are comprehensible even to a child, and towards ideas which are incomprehensible and have no relevance to conduct.

The dualism is a contradiction of the practical, down to earth, unified attitude of the religion of the

Jews, a people for whom a bush could be on fire with the presence of God. It was the Jewish religion, the Jewish insight and genius, unmatched anywhere in history, which, in spite of later corruption and fanaticism, nourished the seed of Christianity. Is there any place in Christianity for the attitude that regards this world as a passing show obscuring the eternal truths? Is it not outrageous to the Christian spirit to attempt to separate the noumenal world from the world of phenomena, to divorce truth from the process of discovering truth? And is it not a way of looking at life that is impossible to reconcile with the activities of science?

The Platonic dualism has misdirected our imagination, so that instead of seeing what we call the spiritual as an aspect of experience in its wholeness, we tend to imagine the spiritual world as self-subsisting, independent of material experience, something we shall reach when we pass into the eternal. From this point of view the material world exists simply to exemplify the spiritual, to illustrate for our poor comprehension *ideas* that exist in the mind of God. As I have indicated, this attitude can be understood— together with the longing for Heaven that went with it—in a people for whom there was no prospect of controlling their environment. Have we any excuse for holding such an attitude today, when, through a union of love and science, we really can abolish poverty and hold back the threats to our life?—when on this very earth we can open the doors to an unimagined freedom?

A critic who has read the above paragraphs continues to put the question: "Is the distinction between noumenon and phenomenon being denied? Surely science knows itself to be dealing only with phenomena and does not presume to say what lies behind phenomena?" In reply, what I would urge is that noumenon-and-phenomenon is a polarity that we invent for the purpose of describing experience. It corresponds closely to mind-and-matter; and there are many other polarities that we use similarly: good-and-evil, subjective-and-objective, positive-and-negative. Now you cannot separate two poles without destroying the meaning or existence of both (or, as in the breaking of a magnet, immediately recreating the polarity in the pieces). Positive has no meaning without its opposite, negative; they are indissolubly bound together. Expressions such as "spiritual world", though convenient to use, are abstractions not implying any independent existence. The only "world" is the one in which we live, move and have our being, the world of persons.*

It is interesting to note that both materialism and philosophic idealism (mentalism, spiritism) start from and imply the dualism; they proceed by denying the

* Perhaps what worries people about the denial of the dualism is the implication that there will be nothing left when the body dies; consciousness (the "spirit") will die with it. This is not a necessary consequence at all. If there is a life after death, I am sure it will be as "whole" as this one—a new kind of unity that we cannot envisage. We may with justification laugh at the idea of the resurrection of the bodies we possess now, but there was more sense in this idea than in belief in the survival of the spirit only. St. Augustine, in one of his many delightful passages, is definite about this. Of the resurrected bodies of the saints he says ". . . those glorified bodies, which are spiritual not because they cease to be bodies, but because they subsist by the quickening of the spirit." And later ". . . God forbid we should believe them to be spirit, or other than substantial fleshly bodies." St. Augustine goes to great trouble to explain how God will collect the dispersed fragments (exhalations) of a man who has been eaten by a cannibal. (*City of God*, Book XIII, Chap. 22; Book XXII, Chap. 20.)

opposite term in the polarity they presuppose. It is not surprising that idealism and materialism necessitate and breed each other.

As for science being concerned only with phenomena, what can such a question mean when it is recognized that "phenomenon" is simply a term in an abstract two-part frame of reference? Even if we accept the everyday definition of the term as an object of perception, do we know exactly what that means? We do not; for the mind—with all its "noumenal" implications—participates in the act of perception. Science is not just a description of the phenomenal world; it is deeply imprinted with the nature of man himself. Again to quote Michael Polanyi "Into every act of knowing there enters a passionate contribution of the person knowing what is being known, and . . . this coefficient is no mere imperfection but a vital component of his knowledge."

Quakerism has always fostered the impulse to serve the practical needs of humanity—to take love and help to suffering people wherever they were. Often it seems that throughout our work there is an implied unity of the spiritual and the material. But there is also a contradictory tendency in a people that has rejected the concrete symbols of faith and looked inward for conviction. It is a tendency to accept the dualism in its worst form and to fill the noumenal world with ill-digested notions. Plato's dualism had at least the merit of being rigorously thought out, but the imagination of some Quaker idealists is liable to be led in a most undisciplined way to any one of a host of notions ranging from a simple pantheism through a range of esoteric philosophies and eastern cults to a modern

Gnosticism or psychological religion based on Jung.* People from other sections of the Christian Church who have met and talked with Quakers have with some justification asked me "What on earth *do* Quakers believe?" The tendency I have described is a deeply regrettable one and there is only one thing that will hold it in check: the recognition that the Society of Friends is fundamentally and irrevocably a *Christian* body of worshippers, as irrevocably so as the Catholic Church. Only the centering of our thoughts on the nature of a person—one who existed in history—will be adequate to discipline our thoughts and check the excursions of imagination into sterility. It may be well to remind Friends of a danger pointed out in a teasing joke coming from the Anglican direction, and therefore perhaps from William Temple, commenting on Quaker claims to mysticism. It is to the effect that Quakerism came out of the Church by schism and got lost in mist.

Much of the implied "mistiness" is an ill-disciplined intellectualism or idealism in which not only "material" experience is given an inferior place, but also the immediate life of the feelings. This is a reflection of a general tendency in educated people. The dualism, implicit and often explicit in much of educational thought and standards of judgement, has resulted in an undue emphasis on logical truth and verbal statement, making it difficult for educated people to accept that there are experiences which do not require or imply verbal "explanations". We might call these experiences "mysteries", but unlike the mystery of the detective

* This implies no disparagement of Jung, who must be one of the greatest men living. His speculations are more imaginative than, for instance, those of Freud, and may in the end prove more fertile. But they are also more open to exploitation.

novel, they do not ask for any solution or explaining away; they should be complete and significant in themselves. When I listen, for instance, to the Waldstein Sonata or to Mozart's Clarinet Quintet, deeply mysterious though they are, I am not experiencing something imperfectly, something that I might be able to get behind and express as an idea, something that has a "meaning" to be revealed after death. To think this way is to do a disservice to music, to take away from its inherent sublimity. In such experiences —and these are among works that have moved me very deeply—I am already in the presence of God himself, God the Creator, though the thought of him need not be conscious in my mind.

Exactly the same applies to our joy in our friends or to the delight and tenderness to which we can be moved by little children. "He who hath seen me hath seen the Father" provides the clue to all deep experience of persons and their creations.

IX

THE WORLD OUR HOME

I HAVE said that Jesus spoke in the language of poetry
It is therefore not surprising that a poet should bring
us nearer than the theologians to an understanding
of Jesus. Such a poet is Edwin Muir. In an introduction
to his collected poems, J. C. Hall writes:

> . . . with Muir . . . we are aware of a wonderful en-
> richment of experience. Today his poetry has, I feel,
> a special significance for us. For we are beginning to
> realize that the problems of our time are ultimately
> the problems of our own deepest nature. It is these
> secret places of the soul which Edwin Muir has ex-
> plored for us. We need his vision, his courage and his
> faith.

In view of what I have said in an earlier chapter
it is significant that—in the words of Kathleen Raine—
"Edwin Muir was a symbolist, concerned with the
expression of the archetypal . . . He belonged to no
church, yet his poetry is steeped in the Christian
vision."*

I want to quote one of his poems in full, but before
I do so I must deal with a criticism that has occurred
to me. The enjoyment and understanding of much of
modern poetry are possible perhaps only to a minority
of the human population and in asking for an understanding of poetry from Friends I am asking for something that might tend to increase the exclusiveness of

* "Edwin Muir—an Appreciation". *The Listener*.

Friends and intensify their apparent intellectualism. What is the answer to this?

In every church that meets the needs of a cross-section of humanity there must be some who have the capacity for disciplined intelligent reflection, and many others—a majority—who have not. The quality of the religious community as a whole will depend—*in part*—on the sensitiveness, imagination, and richness of experience of the minority. In the greater part of the Christian Church the ritual—the recitation of the creed, the celebration of the Mass, the Benediction—conveys, even if inadequately, some of the richness and depth of Christian experience to the wider group. Friends dispensed with ritual and this is one of the reasons, perhaps, why their appeal to the majority has been limited; and unfortunately at the same time they closed other openings to enrichment and sensitization, so that their value to the less intellectual and reflective became still further reduced. We have begun to open the doors, but they are not yet wide enough.

I am not asking for the understanding of a literary scholar or a deliberate student of poetry. I am trying to show how the poet breaks through the limitations of words used in their everyday prose context and, by using a different discipline, discovers new meanings, or rediscovers lost meanings, providing new symbols to replace those to which we have become too used. The poet, struggling in the freedom he has given himself, thus often does what the theologian or religious apologist cannot do or has ceased to try to do. The poet's way of approaching experience need not be confined to those who write poetry. Some of the statements that came spontaneously to the lips of early Friends, often simple folk, were unconsciously poetry, expressing a newly discovered freedom of thought and feeling.

Edwin Muir was an extremely sensitive person who felt in his spirit the impact of the modern world in all its capacity to inflict suffering. He saw the tawdry, the destructive, the hateful, no less clearly than T. S. Eliot:

> Men and bits of paper, whirled by the cold wind
> That blows before and after time
> Wind in and out of unwholesome lungs . . .*

But whereas Eliot seems to have turned for reassurance to a neo-orthodoxy in religion and thus to have created a sort of dualism between life and worship, Muir continued to hold everything together; he saw, so to speak, the maggot-crawling boneyard† of humanity, the horror and the degradation, experienced it all in himself so deeply that he was almost destroyed by it. But he was not destroyed; instead of repudiating evil he assimilated it and transmuted it, made it part of his deepest perception and, in a sense, the foundation of his courage. I feel this most definitely in *One Foot in Eden*‡:

> One foot in Eden still, I stand
> And look across the other land.
> The world's great day is growing late,
> Yet strange these fields that we have planted
> So long with crops of love and hate.
> Time's handiworks by time are haunted,
> And nothing now can separate

* T. S. Eliot: *Burnt Norton.*
† This metaphor is suggested by his early experience of two years of employment in a boneyard at Fairport. See *Autobiography.* (Hogarth, 1954).
‡ Edwin Muir, *One Foot in Eden*, Collection of Poems (Faber, 1956).

The corn and tares compactly grown.
The armorial weed in stillness bound
About the stalk; these are our own.
Evil and good stand thick around
In the fields of charity and sin
Where we shall lead our harvest in.

Yet still from Eden springs the root
As clean as on the starting day.
Time takes the foliage and the fruit
And burns the archetypal leaf
To shapes of terror and of grief
Scattered along the winter way.
But famished field and blackened tree
Bear flowers in Eden never known.
Blossoms of grief and charity
Bloom in these darkened fields alone.
What had Eden ever to say
Of hope and faith and pity and love
Until was buried all its day
And memory found its treasure trove?
Strange blessings never in Paradise
Fall from these beclouded skies.

In this poem there is no repudiation and no false
optimism. We are reconciled to our world as the
proper place for our experience and growth. He
transmits some of his own courage to us, enabling us to
say of our life in this world—as he says at the end of
The Difficult Land:

> . . . how can we reject
> The long last look on the ever-dying face
> Turned backward from the other side of time?
> And how offend the dead and shame the living
> By these despairs? And how refrain from love?
> This is a difficult country, and our home.

Reconciliation to our world is necessary if we are to become of more value to the people in it and if we are to reach a maturity in our personal and social life. If it be said that Jesus thought of the "world" as evil, a place whose clutches his followers were to avoid, it should be emphasized that envy, jealousy and revenge, pride, corruption and hypocrisy had soaked into the social life of his day. Administration and social organization were rotten right through. Jesus was born into an occupied country where the moral degeneration encouraged by occupation was similar to what we have seen in Europe—and perhaps much worse. His teaching about conduct was in the sharpest contrast to the daily practice of perhaps most of his countrymen. The term "lost sheep of Israel" had an intensity of meaning that we can hardly begin to imagine. In spite of all that the pessimists might wish to say, our world is very different, thanks to the leaven of Christianity, the unseen and often unrecognized impulse that has been at work through the centuries. For us to accept the world as our spiritual home is not necessarily to become tainted with its evil and its Admass culture; it is to see the wheat among the tares and to recognize the tares for what they are because Christ opened our eyes—and to accept the tares as a necessary part of our experience.

One further point must be made about reconciliation to our world. It involves the acceptance of (though not acquiescence in) the evil of the world, its suffering and dangers, the seeming crudity and insensitiveness of mankind. It means that we must accept these as the experiences through which we find our way to maturity both as individuals and as a community. But it means

97

also that we become intensely alive to its riches, to what it can contribute to the abundant life that Jesus offered. It asks for the keenest development of the senses and of our capacity to feel and to enjoy. It requires that we should set ourselves free from the last vestiges of the Puritanism that cast doubts on the goodness of the flesh and on the spontaneous expression of joy in living. It should make us intensely alive to beauty, able to see it in its unexpected manifestations as well as in the flowers of spring and the other forms in which we have been taught to expect it.

Recently it was my good fortune to see some of the most fascinating places in the world: the blazing red plains of Ethiopia, its volcanic mountains and start-lingly handsome people; the flashing white limestone hills of Lebanon, covered with cyclamen and the red Adonis flower; the long backbone of Mount Hermon with its snow-covered ridges, lifted as though floating on air above the heat-haze of the Syrian plain; the sea of Galilee, peaceful amid the tense activity of Israel; the coral outcrops of the Red Sea and the islands of the Aegean, seen from the air, a glowing orange ringed with fluorescent green. But I came back to find the view from Great Gable, when the mist unexpectedly lifts, just as exciting. If our senses are dormant, to be transported to other parts of the world will perhaps awaken them; yet it should not be necessary. An artist can see beauty and colour in the ripples on the surface of a muddy creek or in chimney pots against a murky sky. To know and to love our world should, within the limits of our ability, make artists of us all.

X

IN WHAT IS OUR FAITH?

I BEGAN this essay with thoughts about science, because the scientific activities of mankind have proved overwhelmingly successful and I thought there might be something to learn from their success. I will not accept the gloomy impulse evident in so many people, when confronted with achievements of science, to point out how primitive and irrational man remains in many respects, how great is the danger of destruction of mankind, how thoughtlessly and vulgarly the population accepts prosperity, how gullible and almost moronic the public seems in face of television advertising and the more disreputable daily press. All this may be true, but it takes away nothing from what science has given us. We may deplore the craze for speed, but we are glad enough when after leaving London Airport on a dismal winter evening we are able to breakfast in the tropical African sunshine. The development that frightens us also makes possible a hitherto unimagined wealth of experience, experience of the world's interest and beauty and a richly varied experience of people.

We must not underrate the freedom that science has made possible, freedom to move about, to investigate and enjoy, and freedom from a host of daily fears. We must not let the danger of nuclear warfare blind us to the fact that from minute to minute in our daily lives we can move about without fear. The fact that we are so shocked by the toll of death on the roads is a measure of the extraordinary degree of safety that the individual of today has been led to expect in his daily life. To a large extent that safety has been provided by science and technical organization. Our concern about cancer, heart disease and peptic ulcers is a measure of our now enormously increased expectation of life.

It must be recognized that science is taking an increasing proportion of our educational activity; that is inevitable. It is futile to deplore it or to imagine that we can balance it by the addition or intensification of other academic studies; we must educate from within science itself. Our thought and our attitudes, yes, and even our religion, must be enlarged to contain it, not in the sense of restricting it but in the sense of giving it full scope to develop in a culture to which it truly belongs. We must think of it ungrudgingly, generously, if we are not to make of it an enemy and an outsider where religion is concerned. The fact is that, in general, our religion is not big enough to contain it in this sense, because religion speaks in a dying language, because it looks backward and inward rather than outward and forward, and because it is too closely concerned with its own survival.

Religion must become a learner. This implies a reversal of thought. We have commonly assumed that the rest of man's activities must take their cue from religion, fit their activities into the pattern provided by the insight and wisdom of religion. There is a sense in which the opposite is the truth. The statement that the meek shall inherit the earth applies to the Church and to religion as a whole as well as to the individual man and woman. A readiness humbly to learn from the rest of the world's activities instead of an urge to begin by making judgments about them might indeed lead the Church to its true inheritance—the whole of man's endeavour. The Church cannot reach this condition unless it is prepared to set its thinking and its imagination free, by casting off habits that are not appropriate to the age and not essential to the Christian message. The Church may fail to do this. It may retain its present membership, and it may indeed increase it for a while in an age where fear drives people to seek bolt-holes; but the result will be the split-mind, a dichotomy of culture and ultimately the death of religion as we know it.

In what I have written I have spent a relatively small proportion of time thinking about Quakerism. I have mentioned no Quaker worthies. I make no apology for this. Quakerism will not become more vigorous or wholesome by concentration on itself, but by looking outward. The same is true of the whole Christian Church. If I state it in its own accepted terms, the purpose of Christianity is not to save the Church but to know God and enjoy him for ever. This is to know him in every manifestation, to know and enjoy his universe, to see it through the eager eyes and restless imagination of the scientist as well as to feel it through the passion of the artist. Religion is the assertion of what gives meaning and coherence to our community life, of our need for tenderness and enjoyment of each other; but it is also our response to the totality of experience, it is what happens to all our knowledge and experience reaching the intense focus of consciousness at the centre of our being—a point where thinking and feeling unite but where words may fail us. If religion is our response to the totality of experience it should be able to include science as part—a very large part—of its activity. If it cannot (and largely it does not) it is because our religion is small-minded, parochial, turned in upon itself, and for all its apparent certainty, frightened.

It is easy to criticize the blinkered technologist who seems to look at the whole of life through the narrow opening of his gadgetry; and it is not difficult to find scientists who are creative within their own field but insensitive to the world outside. But for many research workers and teachers, science provides a very real fulfilment, an expansion of thought and personality that puts the self-consciously religious person to shame. There was a recent television broadcast which posed the question "What is Life?" in which Professor Swann walked about inside a model of a living cell discussing with various experts the problems of inheritance, of chemical assimilation and molecular reproduction, of virus infection and cancer. I am told that for those who had no foothold in biochemical knowledge the broadcast was not an unqualified success; but for those who knew something of current research—in the chemistry of protein and nucleic acids, the behaviour of mitochondria, phages and viruses—it was an impressive demonstration of the breadth and intensity of the scientific imagination, its creativeness and fertility, of the quiet, yet under the surface deeply exciting, world-wide co-operation—co-operation not in the grinding of an axe but in the search for truth.

Research on the cosmic scale has recently become clouded by international competition in the launching of satellites and space-probes, but here too we are confronted by a rapidly growing challenge to the thought and imagination of the scientist, so that once more one is almost inclined to think of Koestler's description of "sleepwalkers' assurance" when one considers the daring imagination that will tolerate the "continuous creation" of hydrogen nuclei out of nothing,* hitherto unthinkable, to explain the constant density (if constant it is) of a probably expanding universe, and an excess of positive charge, hitherto also unthinkable, to explain the expansion.

The scientific revolution of the seventeenth century took place because man ceased to be preoccupied with making tidy thought-systems within his own mind and began to look at the world, bringing wholesomeness and nourishment to his thought by real experience. The early days of the Royal Society meetings must have been days of great exhilaration and excitement. We in our time have entered a period of equal revolutionary importance and even greater fascination and promise. To those who know what is happening and are not frightened by it, there is a tremendous enlargement of vision, and developments are taking place with far greater speed than in the seventeenth century. As I must emphasize again, this is not a phase of which religious people can afford to be benevolent and condescending spectators, thinking that they have something special that puts all this activity in its place. Organized religion has a way of forgetting its past, of slowly taking notice of scientific knowledge a hundred years late and then pretending that it had assimilated it or foreseen it long before. This is the dishonesty of people who think they share God's omniscence.

* Bondi, Gold and Hoyle, 1948.

The enlargement of vision brought about by the earlier scientific revolution had a rapid effect upon philosophy, politics, religion and literature, and this is evident in the cultural developments of the eighteenth century. The effect upon religion seems to have been more in the outlying activities of religious people than in the citadel of belief, where religion remained narrow and defensive in outlook until, at the hands of T. H. Huxley, it took the beating and discredit it deserved. To many of the scientists of the seventeenth and eighteenth centuries, as well as to writers, the opening up of the tight little world-centred universe of mediaeval cosmology and the later discovery of the microscopic realm brought an enlargement of the vision of God—as Creator. In our time there is reason for a far greater enlargement of vision. If the majesty and mystery of God mean anything to us, they must now mean more than ever before.

The tidy little universe of Dante has gone and now even the sun is of no more significance in our galaxy than is a speck of dust on the floor. And our galaxy, made up of billions of stars, is only a relatively tiny cluster, slowly turning in an immensely greater universe, a probably expanding universe where millions of similar galaxies go hurtling away from each other with ever increasing velocity. In the universe of mediaeval times the earth was served by its satellites. It was the one and only home of God's creatures, and the Church therefore was the only church.* Now we must be prepared to accept that, strewn through all the

* I have been told that Aquinas suggested the possibility of other inhabited worlds, and certainly in later times Tycho Brahe and Giordano Bruno did; but the effect on religion of these speculations was negligible.

galaxies, there may be hundreds of thousands, perhaps millions, of planets where physical and chemical conditions have reached the point at which life becomes possible. If we are the children of God, we are not his only children, if our Christian Church is the church of God, it is not his only church. If we do not face this, then it is only a limited and parochial God that we worship. If we do face it, then we must recognize the need for a greater humility than we have ever yet known.

Humility has to be accompanied by faith. For religious people faith has often consisted in getting into a state of mind in which there is "belief" in some statement, perhaps a creed, which is really incomprehensible or meaningless without a knowledge or understanding of the historical problem or situation in which the statement was first made. Churches, unconsciously Manichean, have sought to plant this kind of faith quickly in the young and to nourish it by exercise and catechism lest the Devil get there first.

What is it that the scientist has faith in? Surely it is in the way he and all his fellow scientists behave when they are doing their job—the way they conduct their work in laboratories, the way they think and test and record and judge. They are so used to it that they take it for granted and forget that it is something men had to strive for and establish. I would suggest that our religious faith too should be faith in a *way*. That should come before everything, before even a faith in God; for how can you have faith in God before you have found the way to know him and to recognize how he speaks? Jesus showed humanity the way; St. John puts into his mouth the words "I am the way . . . no man

cometh unto the Father but by me." He showed us
the way to the rebirth, the release, the redirection, that
enables us to learn and profit by experience. Christians
arguing about the nature of God and his relation to
Jesus have been too much concerned with the existence
of God as though it were a static existence dissociated
from action, so that they have thought of God behind
action instead of God *in* action. They have been more
concerned to prove, assert, establish his *existence* instead of recognizing him in action; though what would
existence be without action?

Faith in the way involves a complete rejection of
the Platonic conception of the divine as "self-sufficient;
being beyond change and having all in itself". It is
inconsistent with Christianity. In the wholeness of
Jesus we *see* God—God whose very nature is to be active,
creative, at work among men. God is known by what he
does; he cannot withdraw from man and from action
because to do so would be to deny his own nature. So
I suggest that our faith should not be in a noumenal
God or in statements about him, but in God-in-action,
in a way of life, a way of learning demonstrated by
Jesus.

Further, to be a Christian is not to have faith in a
set of principles that can be applied to the various
aspects of life, or that can be used as a sort of microscope
to examine and judge our actions. Christianity is
not a set of rules or laws, it is not an ethical or moral
code. Christianity does make a difference to our daily
life, to our ethics and our morals; but the principles
and the ethics are what we see in retrospect; they are
the consequence of Christian inspiration but they are
not what makes us Christians. Christianity is a way

of digesting and assimilating experience, a way of taking experience into ourselves and making it part of our personality. We cannot become Christian simply by applying Christian principles to daily life; if we have entered into the Christian experience our lives will express it; conscious "application" will be a subsidiary though often necessary activity. If we start from the right end, from experience in its depths, we shall be able to move forward to deal with the unexpected situations that now confront us instead of remaining stuck in an anxious consideration of what is or what is not in accordance with Christian principles.

To have faith in the way means, in a sense, that we abandon certainty. The scientist trusts the way he abandons himself to the world. He doesn't say that he must get his beliefs, his pattern of thought, certain and neatly ordered before he approaches new facts. It seems to me that he approaches his work not with security, but a kind of insecurity. He does not reach out for new material to incorporate into an already certain body of fact and theory, but often moves forward with his left foot before his right is firmly set.

I have shown how the great seventeenth century revolution in science took place because men began to be fascinated by the world outside them, and became less concerned with building up within their own minds a world of thought, perfect in mathematical, philosophic or theoretical form. They had to give up the preoccupation with perfection and certainty in order to know the world of nature. They began to see the world, not just afresh, but in a sense for the first time, to see it as an intelligent and perceptive ten-year-old boy sees it, a place of endless fascination and of endless questions. Although the certainty and tidiness of the mediaeval cosmology was shattered for ever, the new scientists moved forward with confidence, a confidence born of a new kind of relationship, a new way of living with nature.

The effectiveness of this new way is the most outstanding fact in the whole of subsequent history. In a more general sense—and therefore in religion—I think that we must abandon the desire for certainty and security if we are able to move anywhere at all.

I have suggested that in the absence of dogma and creed, Friends are well set to move forward towards a new religious activity and vitality. Our search for illumination should be a search for the condition of spirit, the awareness of God at work, that releases us —releases us into a positive, generous, giving attitude to experience, into a knowledge of the abundant life.

I am asking for more life, more vigour, more exuberance, more adventurous confidence. But let us make sure that we produce no counterfeit. In 1938 I met a number of young Nazis visiting England. It was difficult not to be impressed by their clear eyes, confident manner, happy appearance and firm handshake. That experience was useful in that it made it impossible for me ever again to judge by the *appearance* of faith and joy. Both political and religious "faiths" may ride unheeding over the real material of experience.

There is a difference between religion and science that must be pointed out and emphasized in an essay that has sought so much to stress similarities. The difficulties that the scientist encounters may be very great and demand all the intelligence and imagination of which he is capable. But he can close the laboratory door at the end of the day and leave it all behind. The difficulties that we deal with in religious activity are often those that shake us to the core of our being, that pursue us or take us by surprise, that will not leave us alone, that penetrate right through our work and leisure. In religion we try to deal with isolation and loneliness, the most continuous and pervading fear of man. We have to face the inevitability of tragedy, the irremediable loss of people we love, that can be like a limb torn out of one's own body. We have to try to face the reality of even deeper tragedy—known to so many in Europe twenty years ago—of losing parents, children, husbands, wives in circumstances of overwhelming evil or of watching the systematic destruction of personality in circumstances of utter degradation. To those who carry the scars of these experiences it would be a callous insult to offer the possibility of "scientific solutions" or psychological comfort. It is difficult for religion, even at its most clear-sighted and most deeply personal, to face without evasion the worst that has happened in our life-time; yet that is its task. It has to do that as well as to offer to the individual love, tenderness and joy.

The scientist can go ahead on the assumption that no practical problem is insoluble; but personal life that is richly and deeply lived meets unavoidable pain and insoluble problems. Professor Butterfield sees in the movement of historical events "irreducible dilemmas", conditions of "absolute predicament . . . in the very geometry of human conflict".* These are situations from which there is no way out except through yet more evil. We have to face something similar in the

* *History and Human Relations, 1951.* (Collins, 1951).

relationship of persons. Even love, the central concept of Christian action—even love at its best—can break through all the neat organization we provide for it to produce situations for which human wisdom and tolerance are unprepared and inadequate.

We have only to look at the condition of many marriages and at the consequent suffering of children to find examples of the situations I have in mind. The tragedy lies not so much in the fact that mistaken actions or unforeseen developments have led to suffering —human life will never be free from this—but that the persons concerned often do not know how to assimilate the suffering when it comes. It must be clear that religion must do more than merely wait until there is enough understanding to prevent conflict and error. It has to find a means of redemption and renewal— something that, paradoxically, makes use of failure and suffering. Thus, though religion has to learn from science, it must itself be much more than science.

Because we are concerned, in our religious activity, with the experiences that affect so profoundly our whole life, the preparation of ourselves for our task has to be much more complete and whole a preparation than a scientist finds necessary for his work. In all that I have said about the lessons that religion can learn from science, there is nothing that reduces the necessity for worship and contemplation. Before I conclude I want to give an illustration of the way in which I think we should approach the problem before us.

Two years ago a small group of Friends met to consider the problems brought into prominence by the Wolfenden Report—problems first of homosexuality and later those of sexual conduct in general. All but two of us were trained in scientific method—teachers, psychiatrists, research workers. We knew that we had to deal with actions and evidence that to most people were repulsive, and that even in ourselves, who had come voluntarily to investigate these matters, there were disgusts and inhibitions that made it difficult for us to understand the predicament of the offenders against law and convention. We knew that we had to do as Jesus did, to reach out imaginatively to understand. To do this we had to set aside all pre-judgments. We could not know these people if we first of all thought of them as sinners. We had to abandon all those fierce certainties and categorical judgments that people have in the past believed to be inseparable from Christianity, relying only on its revelation of the need of love and of the quality of love that Jesus offered. Casting aside so much, what were we left with? A faith that in the honest search for truth—in so far as it *was* honest—we could not depart from the way of God.

But we had to prepare *ourselves*, for the investigation and judgment of sexual conduct can be deeply coloured by unconscious impulses, and clear-sightedness is difficult to achieve. So our conferences have been preceded by a full-length meeting for worship in which we have been encouraged to face everything in ourselves as well as in the world. Those meetings for worship have been sometimes completely silent yet times of intense activity.

I think I can say that of all the specific group-work I have experienced in the Society of Friends, this has been the most moving, and most convincing in its effect. By abandoning certainty of judgment in an aspect of life where the Church has in the past been most vehemently certain and uncompromising, we reached a deeper certainty and a more creative one. It could not be said that we have reached solutions to what are among the most intractable problems of our time. Indeed we have had to recognize that there are conditions for which no one is responsible and which we can do little to remedy; and that we must all, at least in spirit and imagination, share as Jesus did in body and apparently in defeat, the suffering of our fellows. More than anything else the experience of this work has brought us an understanding of compassion, the need to enter into the lives of others and know how life feels to them.

This experience has been one of growing unity, of intimacy of spirit, of liveliness as well as gravity. It has been to us a revelation. The moment I use this word I think of the way in which the slowly accumulated truths of science are sometimes contrasted, with the "revealed" truths of religion. But is there *any* difference? Only if we are committing ourselves to a dualism and thinking in terms of ideas, or if we are dressing up primitive magic in respectable clothes. There is no fundamental difference if we see supremely in Jesus, as we see sometimes almost equally clearly in the friends we love, the *living* truth—truth as a movement, a process, a continuing action—in a person.

I am often sorry that we were ever called Quakers. Too often the term Quaker—originally a jibe, and meaningless in the modern world—obscures the deeply significant origin of our true name, a name that should inspire and humble us.

> I do not speak of you any more as my servants; a servant is one who does not understand what his master is about, whereas I have made known to you all that my Father has told me; and so I have called you my friends.*

Jesus may not actually have used these words, for the Gospel of John is interpretive rather than a factual record. That does not make them any less significant, for even so they indicate what Jesus had *become* to his followers.

Is the Christian Church outgrowing the attitude of ecstatic adoration and near-idolatry, and will it increasingly recognize what it means to be the companion of Christ in discovery? Friends have in their very name accepted this relationship; we have little excuse for failing to recognize the implications; we have nothing to lose.

I have come to the end of an essay directed to the Society of Friends with hardly a mention of the Inner Light—until this moment. I make no apology for that. I have, in fact, been talking about it all the time. Let me recall another scene in Shaw's *St. Joan*. It is near the beginning; Joan has just joined Robert de Baudricourt and Bertrand de Poulengey in a room in the Castle of Vaucouleurs.

> *Robert.* What did you mean when you said that St.
>   Catherine and St. Margaret talked to you every day?
> *Joan.* They do.
> *Robert.* What are they like?
> *Joan.* I will tell you nothing about that. They have not
>   given me leave.

* John 15, 15.

Robert. But you actually see them; and they talk to you just as I am talking to you?

Joan. No: it is quite different. I cannot tell you: you must not talk to me about my voices.

Robert. How do you mean? Voices?

Joan. I hear voices telling me what to do. They come from God.

Robert. They come from your imagination.

Joan. Of course. That is how the messages of God come to us.

SWARTHMORE LECTURES
PREVIOUS TO 1940

GEORGE ALLEN AND UNWIN LTD

GEORGE ALLEN & UNWIN LTD
London: 40 Museum Street, W.C.1
Auckland: 24 Wyndham Street
Sydney, N.S.W.: Bradbury House, 55 York Street
Cape Town: 109 Long Street
Bombay: 15 Graham Road, Ballard Estate, Bombay 1
Calcutta: 17 Chittaranjan Avenue, Calcutta 13
New Delhi: 13-14, Ajmeri Gate Extension, New Delhi 1
Karachi: Metherson's Estate, Wood Street, Karachi 2
Toronto: 91 Wellington Street West
Sao Paulo: Avenida 9 de Julho 1138-Ap. 51
Singapore, South East Asia and Far East: 36c Prinsep Street